MASTER THE BUSINESS OF MOBILE GIFT WRAPPING

MASTER THE BUSINESS OF MOBILE GIFT WRAPPING

Unleashing Creativity and Convenience

MICHELLE M HENSLEY

Mastering Mobile Gift Wrapping: Unleashing Creativity and Convenience

For more information, email michelle@michellemhensley.com.

ISBN: 979-8-89316-781-8 - Paperback
ISBN: 979-8-89316-780-1 - ebook

CONTENTS

MY STORY

Rolling over in bed after tossing and turning all night, I lay there thinking about how I was a stay-at-home pastor's wife, now widow, and homeschooling mom who hadn't been in the workforce for well over a decade. How was I supposed to support myself and create income? Tears were streaming down my face. I had no one to talk to since my husband had passed away the year prior. Here I was, age fifty-one, trying to figure it all out as anxiety gripped my heart like a rubber band.

During my marriage, I started and ran a nonprofit that fed the working poor. I was also a counselor, but I had worked pro bono, not for profit. However, as a widow, I didn't know how I was going to ask for money or even work for money. I was used to giving it away.

During the first year without Eric, I experienced some personal medical issues because of the stress of the prior two years, from his diagnosis to his passing. He was diagnosed with metastatic melanoma, and it went from stage 3 to stage 4 in thirty days. I was at a run every day for two years, worrying about everything. Eric and I went to a holistic camp to try to heal him naturally, but his cancer was so aggressive that he decided to get chemo at his doctor's suggestion.

It was a whirlwind of all the work it took to support him and take care of him, the children, the church activities, and all the other things, in addition to worrying about my future. What happens to a pastor's wife when the pastor passes away? Now alone, I wanted to stay under the warm blankets, having a false sense of security and not knowing what to do. But life needed to go on.

In July 2015, I interviewed with a company where somebody had graciously offered me a potential position. I was sitting there during the interview, thinking, *I am going to be working sixty hours a week for this five-star company, but I have children grieving at home. I am still homeschooling two of my children and have grandchildren on the way. So there's no way I'm going to be able to do that.*

I knew that taking that job would be contrary to my vision and mission, which was to launch my children in life, whether a career, school, or marriage.

When I was driving home from the interview, I was very discouraged. I thought, *Is there a way I can create a business where I can work when I want and when I can versus when I have to? And would other women want the same thing?*

I just didn't know what to do, so I talked it over with my children.

One of my sons said, "Mom, you had a gift basket company when you were younger. Why don't you do that again?"

I had no idea what I was doing, but in the end, he helped me launch the Nifty Package Co brand. What a great name! *Nifty* means "very good; fine; excellent, capable, stylish and trendy." It was exactly what I was looking for! *Package* encompasses all that we do. As a noun, it means "an object or group of objects wrapped in paper or plastic, or packed in a box." As a verb, it means "present in a particular way." This was a perfect name for the launch of my gift basket business.

Right at the start, one of my daughters-in-love helped me get started. I am telling you, I was terrified to start meeting people and had no idea what to do. My goal was to have me and those working at Nifty working remote from our houses, which wasn't popular when I started in 2015. I just loved the Uber business model, so I modeled my business idea around that.

I think that a gift and curse I deal with is that sometimes, I just launch. Once I make up my mind, whether I know about it or understand the risk or reward or not, I just launch!

I started out making gift baskets mainly for corporations because I knew that bulk purchasing would be better because of volume than sales to individuals, although I sold to anyone who would buy. I did not understand all the important facts of cost of goods, profits, margins, and marketing. I just started. I want you to understand that even if you are afraid and don't know what you are doing, you can learn from my mistakes. What drove me in the beginning was a vision to work when I could, when I was able, and when I wanted. Plus, I love the creative side of business.

I knew that in my own heart and in the hearts of other women—whether those working in corporations, younger moms, or those over fifty—time and family are very important. So, based on this thought, I started to think of the ways this remote working idea would be a good one. It is interesting now, looking back over COVID, to remember that this once frowned-upon idea is now a reality.

I thought, *Is there a way women can work from their homes? Work when they are available and not always have to be at a location?* This was when Uber was still starting, and I loved the concept of remote work, driving when you could and when you wanted, checking in, checking out, and taking care of your family or whatever responsibilities you had outside work.

This business model was unusual, and many people told me it wouldn't work. I felt strongly that I had to try. I asked other women, and hands down, every one of them said, "What a great idea!" Any businessperson or coach said it would not work. But, in my mind, I thought it could work.

This is why so many successful people say your why matters. My why was my children and other women.

When I started Nifty, and for many years afterward, I did not know much about business or how to run it. Nothing. I didn't even know how to pay bills online. My oldest son had to come over, set me up on a budget, and teach me how to set up online payments.

When I lost my husband, I was still unsure what direction I was going. About a year after my husband passed, I hired a finance coach and told him everything that was going on. He told me to get rid of the gift business and start coaching widows.

I replied, "I have no idea how to do that."

"Go find out," he said. "Figure out, come back, and let's talk about it."

After understanding what coaches do and who they are, I found this was a great path for me at that point. I became a board-certified coach in finance, grief, and life. This was a great start to working with widows. I have a full class set up online and have taught it at the local college. However, I started to work simultaneously in the financial services industry because now I had been fully educated in practical financial matters and had become board certified as a financial, life, and grief coach while building Nifty because I needed to have an income. But the Nifty team was a great support, which enabled me to work full-time while growing the business. They were working together, and I was figuring things out. I made every single mistake you could possibly make because I did not understand the real cost of time and money needed to start my own business.

I had been out of the workforce for fourteen years, so I really had no idea how business or marketing functioned. I had been giving away money and food versus asking for money, which you have to do in sales. I'd never correlated sales with asking for money and creating a profit. I didn't understand any of that. Nifty did well my first couple of years, but I absolutely didn't understand profit, let alone how to start and run a business.

Early one morning in 2018, I was up at four a.m. to pray and read my Bible, which I have been doing for well over twenty-five years. I noticed that my van was sitting on the curb outside the house. I thought, *My van is not being used all the time. What could I do to use it more? I make gifts. Could I drive around and wrap gifts? I make corporate gifts and gourmet gift baskets. Why not wrap them too?*

So I put up a gift wrapping service web page, Nifty Package Co Mobile Gift Wrapping Service. And voilà, within about a week, I was wrapping gifts for one of my favorite corporate clients.

He said, "Michelle, I hate wrapping gifts, and I have about twenty-five for my grandchildren. Can you wrap them for me?"

I put every piece of wrapping paper, tape, and all the other supplies and went over and promptly wrapped every gift. The problem was that I forgot to label them, so I had to undo everything and rewrap. Needless to say, I was exhausted, but a new part of my business was born.

About three months later, in March 2019, Too Faced Cosmetics contacted me. They had seen the Nifty Instagram account and asked me to design their wrap for an upcoming event. It was one of the coolest jobs! It was my first big gift design and wrap job. Their Instagram page got over a million likes on our design.

After that job went viral in August 2019, I received a call from a very sweet gal who said she was the estate manager for Kim and Kanye Kardashian. She said, "We've been following your Instagram and would be very interested in you coming out and doing a gift wrap design for Kim and Kanye.

I was still working full-time, but I told my boss that I had this opportunity and asked if I could take the day off. I was transparent about it, and he was gracious in supporting me.

Kim requested eco-friendly wrapping materials, so I gathered all that I had. Then, my local team of about six at the time and I went out to Calabasas, where she and Kanye lived, with a van full of beautiful gift wrap paper Nifty gals in tow. We did several wraps, but Kim was not a fan of the suggestions I made. My whole team was watching me to see how I would handle it.

This was a crossover moment for me. I was so used to giving everything away that I was afraid to ask for money or market my services. And now that I was trying to do that, Kim Kardashian was rejecting design after design. So I walked outside and said, "Lord, you brought me here, and I'm not going home until I make her happy."

I walked back in, approached one of the gals who worked for Kim, and asked, "Do you have any fabric?" She brought me a silky scarf, and I did a *furoshiki* wrap—and Kim loved it! It turned out absolutely stunning. For the next three years, we did her designs and received a top ranking in their magazine, *Poosh*, for our work. Other members of the Kardashian family then hired us, and we did their wrapping. Eventually, we were hired by Justin and Hailey Bieber, who are just a darling couple with an incredible estate team.

Now, the Nifty Package Co team of about fifty wrappers—mostly women with a few amazing men—wrap on a national level and are number one in the mobile gift wrapping space. We are mobile, and all our supplies can service the client on-site at their location, where we wrap their gifts or products. I have a van full of several types of gift wrapping supplies, papers, ribbons, and embellishments that are well-organized and planned. We wrap for families, shut-ins, and corporations for their gifting, book launches, and displays. You name it! Our clients are people who love the look and beauty of the gift wrapping but don't have the time or desire to wrap themselves.

Let me share how I did this!

INTRODUCTION

This book is for anyone who is creative, willing to work, and eager to learn about the art of mobile gift wrapping as a business, not a hobby. I myself was terrified because I lacked the knowledge of how to start a business, let alone grow one.

Why I wrote this book:

1. I want you to see how—with some creativity, a proven business system in a new niche market, and hard work—you can build a business that could create a good part-time job that has the potential to eventually provide your income without business experience.

2. You can do this no matter your age or background. I started at fifty-one and had not worked for over thirteen years in corporate America. I was raising children, homeschooling, and running a nonprofit organization. And I was afraid.

3. With the many tools available today—Canva, Google Workspace, and AI—you can start without experience. So that I don't leave you hanging, I have a free mini course on how to get started on your entrepreneurial journey. Then I have a paid mini course on how to start a mobile gift wrapping business. There are also coaching packages and a full mobile gift wrapping licensing program available. Check out http://michellemhensley.com

I'm a veteran of the $300 billion gifting and $5.4 billion gift basket and mobile gift wrapping industries, and I'm honored that you've decided to enter this fun and rewarding lifestyle.

Even though I'm a longtime gift basket maker, gift wrapper, and gift fulfillment gal, a feeling of joy still washes over me each time I create a new design. You'll feel that same joy as you wrap your first gift—one you get paid for—and I hope the satisfaction will stay with you for many years.

Why Gift Wrapping?

Gift wrapping is timeless. It's also a niche and can be very profitable if done correctly. But first, what is it?

According to Merriam-Webster, the definition of *gift wrapping* is "to wrap (merchandise intended as a gift) decoratively with ribbon or fabric." *Mobile* means you go to the client (whether a business or individual) to wrap their gifts. Or you can pick up their gifts and return them wrapped.

Mobile gift wrapping is on the rise because people don't have the time to create well-wrapped gifts, yet they love the aesthetics and beauty of them. Luxury gifts, or any gifts for that matter, need to be wrapped. I love the rise of the gig economy, but Nifty is different because we serve our customers in person. Someone will answer the phone. According to BusinessWire, the rise of mobile workers in the United States is forecast to increase from 78.5 million in 2020 to 93.5 million by 2024.[1] Consumers want to be engaged with their choice of business so that it is less transactional and more focused on serving clients.

Nifty is also participating in the rise of the desire for convenience in servicing whatever their need is such as Uber, TaskRabbit, or DoorDash. We are similar in that clients can call and order at their convenience, saving the effort and time it takes to decide on, shop, and even deliver beautifully wrapped gifts. People are looking for convenience, and time is an issue. Many work or are busy and would like their gifts wrapped. Many companies want gifts for their board or staff to look amazing and professional. And many companies are outsourcing their work to third parties because of the shortage of time. They save time and money when they don't use their own staff to do the wrapping.

PR firms hire us for on-site brand activations, which are events, campaigns, or interactions companies use to drive client actions. Activations aim to generate brand awareness, build lasting relationships with the audience, and develop client loyalty.

You have influencers and celebrities who want picture-perfect gift wraps that are meant to be photographed. These aren't conversations about money but about look and feel.

This is one of those new opportunities, kind of like milk turned out to be. In the past, milk was consumed primarily in coffee and cereal. And sometimes, it was a mealtime beverage. But, once Starbucks

---

[1] "Mobile Workers Will Be 60% of the Total U.S. Workforce by 2024, According to IDC," BusinessWire, September 1, 2020, https://www.businesswire.com/news/home/20200901005238/en/Mobile-Workers-Will-Be-60-of-the-Total-U.S.-Workforce-by-2024-According-to-IDC.

started selling coffee drinks with milk in them, a new market and demand for milk was created. As a result, milk production increased.

Let me share my four favorite things about this fabulous craft:

1.   Wrapping gifts is fun and rewarding.

Now more than ever, people need joy and hope. I can't bring them hope, but I can inspire them and bring joy by wrapping the gifts that clients have chosen for others. This is key, and it brings both the client and the recipient joy in a difficult and sometimes confusing world.

2.   You can quickly master the steps to create professionally styled designs.

Gift wrapping is a craft, and professional gift wrapping is a greater skill. When you acquire that skill, you can master the art of gift wrapping and create an income as a result. Just like any other skill set, you can master it even if you have really never taken the time to do so in the past. Practice is key!

3.   Not too many people have started their own gift wrapping business. So you can be the first in your area, just like how Uber started!

This is one of these new opportunities that is in the beginning stages. With the rise of the value of convenience—not only for the professional mobile gift wrapper but also for the client who is hiring them—this will be a market that continues to grow.

4.   You can start in your home or garage and use your own vehicle, which keeps costs to a minimum.

The blessing is that you're able to start with very little. By the end of your first Christmas holiday season with your new business as a mobile gift wrapper, you'll have enough profit to pay off any expenses related to your launch, which makes it lucrative, easy, and convenient.

What This Book Covers

By now, I'm sure you're excited and ready to learn all about the business of mobile gift wrapping, so let me share what you can expect from this book.

You'll learn what it's like to wake up each day and operate a mobile gift wrapping business. A gift wrapping designer's life (*designer* is the formal title given to a person who designs and wraps gifts) is much different from a traditional office worker's experience. Each day brings new opportunities, and with those opportunities comes the ability to positively impact other people's lives while making more money than you might make at a regular job. Chapter 1 explains the art and business of having a mobile gift wrapping business. Chapter 2 teaches you how to embrace the role of your new business, understand client pain points, and set yourself up for success.

You'll learn the pros and cons of being a gift wrapping business owner and what it takes to be successful. This includes knowing what to expect each day, how much money you need, how much you can earn, and how to let your family know about your plans so they're supportive and become your biggest cheerleaders. You'll also learn how to market your new adventure. All of this will give your confidence the boost it needs, and you will succeed quickly.

Chapter 3 covers the supplies and essential tools needed for success. Chapter 4 shares some good tips on all things involved in actually wrapping gifts professionally. In Chapter 5, you'll learn how to grow your mobile gift wrapping business. Chapter 6 offers you sales skills and forty ways to market your gift wrapping business. Chapter 7 explains some of the benefits and challenges of being mobile so you can be prepared.

Finally, and best of all, you can take my intensive mobile gift wrapping online training at http://michellemhensley.com in order to receive more comprehensive hands-on instruction and the support you need to make your first professional gift wrap! The course will prepare you for success on your own terms. So whether you're wrapping gifts part-time or full-time, each step will be a smooth and easy process.

Let me be the first to congratulate you for choosing this exciting journey. Are you ready to enter the world of wrapping gifts?

Let's become a mobile gift wrapping boss!

Understanding the Art and Business of Gift Wrapping

G ift wrapping has a history and cultural significance.

In fact, it has a rich history that dates back to ancient civilizations. In China, gifts were wrapped in decorative paper as a symbol of good luck, while in Japan, a similar practice, called *tsutsumi*, involved wrapping gifts in fabric. Paper wrap was less common due to its expense, so fabric was used instead. There's a difference between *tsutsumi* and *furoshiki*, with the former being the original wrap and the latter being used to carry bathing items. The Japanese wrap gifts beautifully and with purpose, using materials like bamboo, paper, fabric, and leaves to create unique and artistic packages.

In Korea, traditional gift wrapping is called *bojagi*, which is a beautiful square piece of silk that is wrapped around gifts. In the Western world, gift wrapping became popular during the Victorian era, with people using tissue paper, lace, ribbons, and even pressed flowers to adorn their gifts. The monetization and standardization of gift wrapping began in the early twentieth century with the introduction of preprinted decorated paper and the rise of department stores. Today, gift wrapping has become an art form, with people using various materials and techniques to make their gifts look beautiful.

Receiving a beautifully wrapped gift is exciting, and the surprise brings joy no matter how small the gift may be. The way a gift is presented is important to not only the giver but also the recipient. It shows that the giver cares about the recipient's experience and took the time to make the gift special. Think about when you have ordered a product from Amazon that comes in a beat-up box. That is fine for some things, but not for a gift. I think shipping a gift from an Amazon warehouse to the recipient or yourself is so convenient. But it takes away the thoughtfulness of your gift. And really, in our hearts, we know that not much thought went into the gift.

But what about when you order from Apple? I don't know about you, but I save their boxes to use in the future. The experience of unwrapping the package to get the treasure inside is delightful. Now consider what it would be like if you take the Amazon gift, wrap it beautifully, send it to the recipient, and go the extra mile with a handwritten note. Isn't that a lovely thought?

A Few Successful and Notable Gift Wrappers through the Ages

Gift wrapping may be a relatively obscure art form to the uninitiated, but it boasts a rich history and has its own legendary artists whose innovations inform the way we give gifts today.

One of the earliest pioneers of gift wrapping was Louis Prang, who popularized the use of decorative paper and cards for gift giving in the late nineteenth century. His work paved the way for the modern greeting card industry and inspired others to explore the art of gift wrapping.

Another notable figure was Joyce Hall, the founder of Hallmark Cards. Hall played a significant role in shaping modern gift giving culture, including the development of innovative gift wrapping designs. His company's success has made him one of the most successful gift wrappers in the world.

Ryoji Matsuoka, a Japanese gift wrapper and author, is renowned for his intricate origami-inspired wrapping techniques. His work has inspired many others to explore the art of gift wrapping, and he has written several books on the subject.

Vivian Kistler was a master picture framer in both the US and the UK. Because she was so good at that craft, she began to master gift wrapping and eventually became an instructor who trained countless individuals in the art of gift wrapping. Her creative and elegant designs have made her a respected figure in the industry.

Shiho Masuda, a very famous and well-known Japanese gift wrap artist, has elevated gift wrapping into an art form with her innovative and elaborate designs. Her intricate techniques have garnered international attention, making her a standout figure in the world of gift wrapping. Shiho takes those who want to increase their knowledge about the art of gift wrapping to her hometown of Ehime, Japan. Participants indulge in a world of handmade paper, traditional Japanese crafts, and the art of gift wrapping. They visit papermaking ateliers and other factories and studios, meet artisans and craftsmen, and learn the history, philosophy, and techniques of gift wrapping, all while enjoying the culture, food, and sights. I would absolutely love to take this adventure!

The Psychology of Gift Giving

People feel very loved when they receive a well-thought-out gift. It also gives pleasure to the giver, builds trust, and enhances social connections. The most important part of gift giving is the person receiving the gift. So when wrapping a gift, I think about that person, whether it is a joyous occasion or even a sad one.

Effective gift wrapping stops the recipient in their tracks, gets their attention, and creates a connection with them. For me, the wrapping conveys that the gift is a luxury item, even if it's a pair of socks that are beautifully wrapped. How about a chocolate bar wrapped in a Japanese paper envelope?

I was invited to an event for businesswomen with high net worths who started, bought, and sold businesses. In my mobile gift wrapping course, I teach the importance of bringing a gift whenever you attend an event. For the businesswomen, I wrapped a wish paper and organic chocolate in two different types of complementary Japanese paper and finished it off with a fabric bow. It was an elevated look and feel! Everyone loved it, and it set me apart. Plus, it enabled me to communicate what I do in my business. Whether it's a business or personal gift, presentation creates several feelings, and that is what you want to help create.

The act of giving a gift activates the brain's reward center and triggers the release of dopamine, a neurotransmitter associated with pleasure and happiness. In turn, dopamine creates positive emotions and sparks a connection between the giver and the recipient. That starts to build a good feeling between both parties. A gift is a symbol of care, love, and thoughtfulness for the recipient is created by both parties as mentioned above, pleasure and happiness.

I love when the time comes for me to wrap or think about a gift. I enjoy the feelings and care I have for the person receiving it, who will be delighted when the gift is presented and opened. I happen to have gift giving as a love language. I love giving and receiving gifts—especially cards that have been handwritten with love and care. I have a drawer full of important cards that I have received over the years. Now, as you spend more time on the gift wrapping side—or, in this case, selling the art of gift wrapping—it will mean even more to you because you took the time to help someone wrap a beautiful gift that they are giving someone.

Nifty Package Co has had many men come in or call us, asking us to wrap a gift for a significant other. What great pleasure it is when I personally thank these individuals who treasure and value us in helping them bring a gift to life. Basically, it's a gift for their recipient, us helping the giver and a gift for me (because I wrapped the gift).

To learn about how to give gifts based on your recipients' love language, go to https://nifty-package-co.squarespace.com/blog/the-5-love-languages-of-gift-giving.

Something to consider is making sure the gift is appropriate for the recipient. Meaning, do you have a relationship with them, or is it business? Be wise about the recipient's feelings. Some people may not want a gift. And some may have a feeling of being "bought." Just consider that.

Traditional Gift Wrapping Was Originally in Upscale Stores

Traditionally, gift wrapping was done in local stores—especially the high-end ones. You used to be able to go into a luxury store, such as Nordstrom or Bloomingdales—or for those of us who are a little past the middle, Bullocks or Robinsons—and they would have a gift wrapping mini service shop where they would wrap the gifts for you in their brand wrap. Or you could purchase the wrapping there.

It's not like that anymore. Beautiful paper is easy to find, but someone to wrap them is not. There are a few stores that supply small gifts and all the supplies needed to wrap them beautifully. Now, things, times, and seasons have changed. People don't go to the malls like they used to, and they don't have the same extra time. As an on-the-go mobile gift wrapper, you bring both freedom and beautiful wrapping to your potential client. That is why this is a new opportunity for business. Mobile gift wrapping will be sought out more and more, especially because of the rise of crime in the high-end malls and stores. People will continue to order online, then bring in a gift wrapper to finish the job.

The Most Successful and Well-Known Mobile Gift Wrapping Businesses

Mobile gift wrapping businesses, which offer on-the-go gift wrapping services, may vary in terms of their success and presence across the United States. While it's challenging to determine the most successful ones definitively, here are a few notable mobile gift wrapping businesses in the country:

Nifty Package Co: Founded by Michelle Hensley, Nifty Package Co is a unique mobile gift wrapping business that offers a comprehensive guide on how to start and run a successful mobile gift wrapping business. With a focus on providing high-quality gift wrapping services, Nifty Package Co has established itself as a go-to resource for individuals and businesses looking to elevate their gift-giving experience. It's also known for its luxury gourmet gift baskets, corporate gifts, and gift fulfillment services.

Wrap It Up: Based in Los Angeles, California, Wrap It Up provides professional gift wrapping services for various occasions, including weddings, corporate events, and personal gifts. It offers on-site wrapping services at events and parties, ensuring that gifts are beautifully wrapped and ready to be cherished.

The Gift Wrap Company: In addition to offering wholesale gift wrapping supplies, The Gift Wrap Company also operates a mobile gift wrapping service. It provides on-demand gift wrapping services for events, parties, and corporate functions, making it easy for individuals and businesses to enjoy professional gift wrapping services without having to leave their premises.

Wrapistry: Based in Houston, Texas, Wrapistry offers personalized gift wrapping services for individuals and businesses. It provides on-site gift wrapping at events, as well as pickup and delivery options, ensuring that gifts are wrapped and delivered with utmost care and professionalism.

Gifted Wrapper: Serving the San Francisco Bay Area in California, Gifted Wrapper specializes in providing professional gift wrapping services for various occasions, including weddings, birthdays, and holidays. It offers both on-site wrapping services and pickup and delivery options, making it easy for individuals and businesses to enjoy beautifully wrapped gifts.

Wrap It Up Mobile Gift Wrapping: Based in Atlanta, Georgia, Wrap It Up Mobile Gift Wrapping offers on-demand gift wrapping services for individuals and businesses.

These are just a few examples of mobile gift wrapping businesses in the United States. The success and availability of such services may vary depending on location and demand in specific areas. It's always a good idea to research and check for local mobile gift wrapping services in your desired location for the most up-to-date information. This way, you can see any competition and make sure your services are unique. Don't forget to read some of the comments from their clients.

Let's Talk Numbers

According to recent market research, the global gift wrapping products market size was valued at USD $17.84 billion in 2022 and is expected to reach USD $31.97 billion by 2031, growing at a compound annual growth rate (CAGR) of 6.7 percent during the forecast period (2023–2031).[2] This significant growth is driven by the increasing demand for environmentally friendly gifting options as consumers become more conscious of the ongoing green movement and the impact of their gift-giving practices on the environment.

The term *gift wrapping products* refers to various materials and instruments used to wrap, adorn, and improve the aesthetic appeal of gifts. These products include present boxes, gift bags, ribbons, bows, tissue paper, gift tags, and other embellishments. The most common form of wrapping material is gift wrapping paper, which is a paper used to conceal the contents of gifts by wrapping them in a rectangle.

I think about when I was younger and Nordstrom was the place to receive a gift from. Gifts were known for their shiny yet matte-looking silver box with that incredibly luxurious ribbon. That was the gift to open! That's the feeling you give when you beautifully wrap a gift for someone. That's the gift they want to open.

The growth of the gift wrapping products market is expected to be driven by several factors, including the increasing popularity of online shopping, the growing trend of gifting, and the increasing demand for sustainable and eco-friendly products.

---

[2] "Design Group in Numbers: as reported in our FY24 annual results," Design Group, accessed July 10, 2024, https://www.thedesigngroup.com/group-by-numbers/.

Additionally, the market is expected to be fueled by the growing popularity of gift cards and the increasing demand for unique and personalized gift wrapping solutions.

Finally, people appreciate the convenience of having gifts professionally wrapped, especially if they are busy or want to add an extra touch to their presents. Offering a mobile service could appeal to those who prefer to have the wrapping done at their location. If you want to gauge the demand, market research in your specific area would be beneficial.

The gift wrapping market is a part of the larger gifting industry, which includes retail, e-commerce, and specialty gifting services. The demand for professional gift wrapping services exists across various sectors, including retail stores, e-commerce platforms, event planning, corporate gifting, and personal services. The market can fluctuate based on seasonal trends, such as holidays and special occasions. Additionally, there is potential for growth in providing specialized or custom gift wrapping services to cater to specific needs and preferences.

Do You Have What It Takes?

Whether you have lots of entrepreneurs in your family or you're the first one who has expressed a desire to start a business, the mobile gift wrapping business is right for you if you have a burning passion for creating beautiful gifts wrapped by hand, making people happy, and earning money all at the same time. When people enter the mobile gift wrapping business, they think that creativity is all they need to succeed. But they soon find out that there's more to it than just putting paper on a gift. That's only part of the puzzle.

Successful mobile gift wrapper entrepreneurs share five essential traits.

Creative flair: If you sew, scrapbook, knit, crochet, or enjoy crafts of any kind, wrapping gifts would be a natural fit for you. Designing is calming, yet it brings out your energy each time you prepare to make something new.

Organization: Keeping all your products, supplies, and tools in place is essential so that you spend your time making beautifully wrapped gifts rather than looking for misplaced items. A little disorder is okay. We're all known to leave a mess now and then. But successful designers make a conscious habit of tidying up to prevent complete chaos.

Patience: It will take a bit of time to become proficient in designing and creating professionally styled wrapped gifts, so be ready to practice, practice, practice. Anyone can throw paper and a bow on a gift, but your mission is to slow down and skillfully master the art of gift wrapping so you can charge a premium.

Outgoing nature: To be successful, you'll need to meet new people and cultivate clients. A genuine smile, a great attitude, and a fun-loving spirit make networking easy and enjoyable.

Determination: Things won't always go your way, and sometimes it may seem that more is going wrong than right! The will to succeed is a valuable and powerful trait. Every designer knows that with each success, you get closer to the finish line. That reality is what keeps us moving forward.

How Much Money Can You Make?

The good news about wrapping gifts is that the earnings potential is huge. You have the ability to earn a significant amount of money when running your mobile gift wrapping business on a part-time basis. If you leap into full-time designing, your revenue can be even more rewarding.

Let's look at some numbers.

First, let's assume that a part-time schedule is twenty hours per week. Next, we'll estimate that half of this schedule (ten hours) will be dedicated to designing, while the other ten hours are for non-design tasks, such as deliveries and marketing.

A gift takes about ten minutes to wrap once you master the basic technique. So, in a four-hour period, you can produce about twenty-five wrapped gifts.

10 minutes for each wrapped gift x 60 minutes = 6 wrapped gifts

6 wrapped gifts per hour x 10 hours = 60 wrapped gifts

The current average retail price for a single wrapped gift is $25. That gives you an estimated weekly gross income of $1,500. Multiply $1,500 by fifty-two weeks, and your projected yearly revenue is $78,000. That's a nice sum for part-time designing!

Now, let's look at the full-time potential. Since we based the part-time schedule on twenty hours per week, let's base the full-time schedule on forty hours. In this case, we'll determine that thirty hours are dedicated to designing.

10 minutes for each gift wrapped x 60 minutes = 6 wrapped gifts

6 wrapped gifts per hour x 30 hours = 180 wrapped gifts

When you apply the same $25 average retail price for a single wrapped gift to this equation, your projected weekly gross income is $4,500. Multiply $4,500 by fifty-two weeks, and your projected yearly revenue is $234,000.

Keep in mind that these projections are gross income amounts, which means that the costs for products and supplies to make wrapped gifts haven't been deducted. That deduction is known as start-up capital, which is the money you invest in the business before you earn income.

How Much Will It Cost?

Today's mobile gift wrap designers spend between a few hundred dollars to several thousand dollars to start and grow their mobile gift wrapping businesses. As you sell the service of wrapping gifts, you'll make money, of course. You'll use some of that money to buy additional products to design more wrapped gifts. You'll sell a wrapped gift, make money, and repeat the process. The basic idea is to buy products and supplies at a reasonable cost, and sell your wrapping service at a higher price to earn a profit. You will purchase most of your supplies from Nifty, or we will send you a list of suppliers so that consistency, luxury, and quality are the same. Plus, we are able to purchase for a better price.

Don't quit your day job yet! There are many designers who have excelled at their craft and are earning their living exclusively through selling their mobile gift wrapping services, but it takes time to reach this point. What makes them successful is patience and determination. If you can balance a knack for designing with a talent for getting orders, you'll soon be ready to enjoy success yourself.

Does the earnings potential motivate you to get started? It's a big part of what convinces people just like you to begin a mobile gift wrapping business, and this book provides ideas, tips, and insider secrets to keep you on track for success. Let's move on and get our hands dirty—let's wrap our first gift!

Embracing Mobile Gift Wrapping as a Business

When you decide to start your own mobile gift wrapping business, your life can change for the better, both personally and professionally. You'll create beautifully wrapped gifts that delight your friends, family members, and clients. You'll experience the pride of owning your own business. And best of all, you'll earn income from doing what you love and be part of a dynamic group of creative people.

Follow along as I get into the nitty-gritty of how to actually set up your new business opportunity. We will cover naming your business, setting up your workspace, practicing, pricing, marketing, and getting supplies to start with.

A Day in the Life of a Mobile Gift Wrapper

Every gift wrapper has one common trait: we wake with a smile, eager to get into the workspace (also known as the design studio) to begin our daily designing.

Does that sound like the life for you?

This is how Skye Taylor starts her day. She's the proud new owner of Stylish Mobile Gift Wrapping by Skye, which she started just six months ago. We're going to learn all about a gift wrapper designer's day through her eyes, and she'll stay with us through the entire course. Many of Skye's tasks will go smoothly, but you'll see in future lessons that not everything goes as planned. She'll hit a few snags, but she'll recover by implementing a Plan B and sometimes a Plan C.

Skye is determined to succeed with her mobile gift wrapping business. She spends much of her time thinking about her next design and brainstorming ideas for how to improve her business. This morning, she woke up very excited, visualizing how she'll wrap with gold-sparkle-and-dusty-pink gift wrapping paper with a gray velvet one-and-a-half-inch ribbon to be delivered later that day to her first client.

Skye sets all the items for the gift wrapping job on a table in the garage she turned into her design studio. She'll get started right after breakfast, a routine she follows every day because she's already learned that following a schedule makes her more productive. It's easy to lose track of time when she's doing something she enjoys.

Skye's gotten good at splitting her time between design work and administrative tasks. The design space is where she puts her creative skills to the test. Her office space consists of a desk, chair, and computer. That's where she writes orders, calculates profits, and decides how she will market her gift wrapping business.

Skye understands that being her own boss and working from home doesn't mean she can be lazy. In fact, it means she has to work even harder to succeed since there's no one else to help her. Scheduling her days in advance helps her get organized.

Here's what Skye's schedule looks like today:

Morning

6:00 a.m. Skye wakes up, gets family members out to school and work, and eats breakfast.

7:30 a.m. She enters the design studio and checks voicemail and her website for overnight email orders or any quote requests that might have come in.

8:00 a.m. It's time to begin creating her wrapped gift requests and completing orders from the day before.

10:30 a.m. Skye checks her inventory to make sure her paper, special double-sided tape, and other supplies are available for new orders.

11:00 a.m. Before lunch, she makes some phone calls to follow up on referrals from her customers and get more business.

Afternoon

12:00 p.m. Is it lunch time already? Skye sits down for thirty to forty-five minutes to enjoy her meal, knowing that this is the only time it's okay to look at the news and check her business Instagram account. (We'll discuss this later.)

1:00 p.m. Skye reenters the studio to continue making custom-ordered wrapped gifts and trying new options that separate her style from other designers. As a new business owner, she will drive through the high-end streets where her potential clients are and drop off postcards or mailers, which is a part of her marketing strategy, in order to meet people and market her gift wrapping business.

3:30 p.m. Once Skye is finished with her current gift wrapping project, she packs the wrapped gifts into boxes for delivery or shipment. If the gifts are heading to local addresses, she prepares to make deliveries by car, then plans ahead with carrying her cards, referral postcards, or newsletter to drop off for any potential client.

4:30 p.m. When she returns, Skye checks her Facebook page to make sure it's up to date, making changes as necessary, and setting up her mobile shop for the next day's event.

5:00 p.m. Another productive design day ends. Skye sweeps and organizes her workspace to prepare for the next day's tasks.

There are some things not mentioned that are also part of Skye's world. Networking, meeting clients for lunch, and ordering products could be part of her day, and the same will be true for you as you enter this dynamic industry. No two days are alike. So, if variety makes you happy, making wrapped gifts is for you!

Understand the Client's Pain Points and Offer a Solution

The number-one reason professional gift wrappers are hired is that the giver does not like or want to do the wrapping. The second reason is that they don't have the time. And third is that they don't know how to wrap well, so it is much easier to hire someone to do the work. In a corporate setting, time, staffing, and creativity are the three most important factors.

Gift-giving doesn't need a special occasion; it's a thoughtful way to express love and gratitude anytime. Despite the distance, sending gifts is easy with shipping options. Remember, the essence of a gift truly shines through its presentation.

During busy times, especially when gifting multiple people, professional wrapping services can be invaluable. Whether the need comes from a lack of skill or time, these experts ensure each gift is wrapped beautifully and ready for any event.

Still unsure about professional gift wrapping? Consider these benefits:

Convenience: It saves time during hectic seasons. Professionals handle the wrapping while the giver focuses on other festive preparations.

Suitable and beautiful wrap and ribbon: Professional gift wrappers have access to a wide range of wrapping materials suitable for any occasion, ensuring gifts always look their best.

Professional gift wrapping offers several advantages that enhance the overall gifting experience:

- **Impressive presentation:** A professionally wrapped gift stands out with its visual appeal, making a strong, positive impression.

- **Stress reduction:** For those who find gift wrapping challenging, professional services ensure a stress-free experience with beautifully wrapped results.

- **Creativity and customization:** Experts provide a variety of wrapping styles and personal touches, making each gift unique and tailored to the occasion.

- **Environmentally friendly options:** Many services offer sustainable wrapping materials, combining elegance with eco-consciousness.

These benefits contribute to making gifts memorable and show the recipient that thought and effort were put into their present.

You are the solution. You are professional, experienced, and able to work a lot quicker than they can for a fee.

Your story is the story of how you learned about gift wrapping and came to want to work for yourself. Learning to lead this way is what is next.

The advantage for the business is that all the wrapping is done in an organized fashion. The gift wrapper has learned about creativity and how to market to corporations. Corporations can hire us to serve their clients, such as CBRE hiring us to come into their lobby and wrap for their leasees. How about a hospital hiring the gift wrapper to come in and wrap for their staff to help ease a burden? How about a company hiring us to wrap all the board of director or influencer gifts? It takes off their plate the responsibility to make the gifts perfect for recipients or investors.

Advantages to Both Individual and Corporate Wraps

In regard to an individual wrap, you will carry all your items with you. You will communicate effectively and set up shop in their home or garage, which is my preference. The timer starts the minute you start wrapping your gifts, not when you're unloading. You get to know the individual. Sometimes they own a business, and there's just an open door to possibly gain more business. Plus, you get to meet a number of wonderful people!

We work in celebrity homes. We work in the homes of shut-ins. We work in homes with families that have children. It's a cool job!

Many times, you'll work alone in these situations, so you get better and you get faster. I still go out a lot because we're so busy during the holidays. Many times, there is a team of two or three, depending on how many gifts there are or who the giver is. When I do a celebrity wrap, the client could want the same look and feel on three to four hundred gifts. Then I definitely have a team with me, and it's all planned—the look and feel, the paper and embellishments. It's all prepared ahead of time as much as possible.

When it comes to on-site corporate work, there are a few ways this works. It is usually planned a few months in advance, so all the communication and marketing materials go out to the event's attendee recipients. We show up with all our supplies, people line up with their gifts, and we wrap on-site. This is more of a creative time, and it doesn't necessarily involve a predesigned look and feel. We bring several different types and styles of wrapping paper, ribbon, and embellishments because we could have somebody who is Jewish, somebody who wants a traditional Christmas fashion, somebody who likes trendy looks, or somebody who likes traditional wrapping paper. We take materials for all of these wraps with us to our individual and corporate jobs. A great question to ask ahead of time is, What is your preference?

An individual or a corporation can actually ship you gifts and have you wrap, then send the wrapped gifts to the client or recipient. You can wrap a hundred gifts in the same kind of wrap for this situation. You can also go do this at the client's office. Or you can go to their location or home, pick up the gifts to be wrapped, take them back to your studio, and then return them wrapped.

Both corporate and individual clients are important, and both reach out all the time.

Setting up Your Schedule for Success

Determining your set work schedule in a home-based business is a very important part of the process. The question becomes, Are you creating a hobby, or do you want a lucrative small business? I always teach to begin with the end in mind. It's a quote and principle taught by the famous author Stephen Covey in his famous book, *The 7 Habits of Highly Effective People.*[3]

What do you really want to do? Your answer will help you determine your schedule.

Working at home offers many benefits. Do you feel it's the ideal place for you? It is for many mobile gift wrappers. But there's one thing you must master before you begin setting up an in-home workspace, and that's *discipline*.

The core of being able to work from home is discipline, focus, and a good schedule you can commit to.

How tempted will you be to watch television, do the laundry, or talk to friends on the phone rather than maintain your business during the hours you establish as work time? Can you concentrate on business without having anyone else to talk to? Will you trade your pajamas every morning for clothes that reflect your professionalism? Wearing a business suit isn't necessary; however, casual clothing, such as a shirt and slacks, is an appropriate uniform when working in this environment.

A simple quote that I repeat to myself regularly is:

"Starve distractions, feed focus." —Tim Ferris[4]

Distractions are common when working at home. You may think that doing a few personal things around the house isn't a big deal, but think again.

---

[3] Stephen Covey, *The 7 Habits of Highly Effective People* (New York, NY: Simon and Schuster, 1989).
[4] Tim Ferriss, *The 4-Hour Workweek* (London, UK: Ebury Press, 2011).

I have a very disciplined life, but I will take breaks when I need to. I get up very early, read my Bible, pray, work out or walk, then go to work! I eat lunch and take a tea or coffee break around one thirty or two p.m. I work in spurts. I might sit at the computer for forty-five minutes to an hour to focus on client work, do lead generation, write blog articles, and watch training videos. I never stop learning, and neither should you.

Now that you're a business owner, it's important to stay focused on your mission, which is creating a dynamic mobile gift wrapping business that leaves clients happy, creates referrals as a result, and makes your life personally and professionally rewarding. If you can do this, then setting up a workspace in the same place you live is for you. Once in a while, if I truly need a break, I close up my shop, take a walk by the beach, or curl up to watch a movie.

A Good Set of Steps

Jim Rohn said, "Let your learning not just lead to knowledge but action."[5]

- Keep and maintain a routine, set office hours, and repeat daily. Get up at the same time every day and know that you are growing a business.

- Have clear boundaries for yourself and your family. However, prioritize your family so they don't feel neglected.

- Take a break when you need to, take a walk, sit outside, and lay everything down—because once in a while, you need that break.

---

[5] Jim Rohn according to "Don't let your learning lead to knowledge . . .," Goodreads Quotes, accessed July 10, 2024, https://www.goodreads.com/quotes/213176-don-t-let-your-learning-lead-to-knowledge-let-your-learning.

- Communicate to others that you really are in business, and make sure you stick to that.

- Stay focused by making a short list of things that need to be done.

- Stay connected. Networking (we will talk more about this) is a great way to get out of the house and feel like you're a part of a business community.

Now that we have that out of the way, let's move on to some fun stuff!

How to Choose the Right Name for Your Business

Ultimately, the business name you choose depends on your long-term vision for your mobile gift wrapping business. If you plan to keep it small and personal, your personal name might work just fine. But if you have aspirations to grow and build a distinct brand, a more creative approach might be better. You might be surprised at how your business can grow. Also, you may plan on selling it later, so choosing a catchy, memorable name that reflects your brand is important to consider.

Choosing the perfect name for your mobile gift wrapping business is an important step!

Five Key Things to Consider

1. Make it memorable and catchy:

- You want a name that sticks in people's minds and is easy to recall.

- Consider rhythm, rhyme, or wordplay to make it more memorable.

2. Make sure it reflects your brand:

- The name should give a sense of what your business offers.
- For a gift wrapping business, consider words like *gift*, *wrap*, *bow*, *ribbon*, *flourish*, *beautiful*, or *creative*.

I chose Nifty Package Co because the term *nifty* means stylish or smart, *package* encompasses everything we do, and *Co* is for corporation I knew I didn't want to be a sole proprietor. I wanted to grow the business. But in this situation, since my desire was to eventually sell Nifty, I did not put my name on it. I recommend the same for you if that's also your goal. But if you're a sole proprietor, you can. It just makes it harder for someone to take over later.

3. Make sure it's easy to spell and pronounce:

- Avoid complicated spellings or phonetics that might confuse potential customers.
- You want people to be able to find you easily through word of mouth or online searches.

4. Choose a name that's unique and stands out:

- Conduct a quick trademark search to avoid infringing on existing businesses. This is very important and should be done first after you decide your name. Skipping this step could result in receiving a scary cease-and-desist letter, and no one wants that!
- Aim for a name that's unique enough to make you memorable.

5. Check the domain and social media availability:

- Check for domain name availability (your www).

- Check the social media handles of your chosen name. Do a search using the terms *mobile gift wrapping* and *gift wrapping services*, and see the different names.

Brainstorming Exercises to Help You Choose a Name

- **Mind-mapping:** Start by writing your main idea in the center of a page, then draw branches to sub-ideas, connecting related thoughts with lines to visually map out your brainstorming in an organized, easy-to-follow way.

- **Thesaurus technique:** Use an online thesaurus to find synonyms and related words for your chosen keywords. I love thesaurus.com and wordhippo.com.

- **Combine and create:** Play around with combining words, using prefixes or suffixes, or even creating a new word altogether.

- **Look at your competitors:** Look up your competitors' names—not to copy but to see who is ranked first on Google. Analyze why that might be. Many times, the top-ranked companies have the easiest names to remember and pronounce.

- **Know your clients' stores:** Make a list of companies that your ideal client might purchase from that have nothing to do with mobile gift wrap. Where do they shop? What are they drawn to? This could be places like Lululemon, Starbucks, Nordstrom, Coach, Ralph Lauren, etc. Sometimes, seeing a theme in the brands they purchase from will give you ideas about how to choose a brand name.

- **Get feedback:** Run your shortlisted names by friends, family, or potential customers for their honest opinions.

- **Say it out loud:** Listen to how it sounds. Could someone understand what you're saying over the phone? Would you find yourself spelling it out for everyone? Now, write it down on paper. How does it look in your handwriting? All of these tactile experiments will guide you to the right business name.

Remember, the best name is one you love that reflects your mobile gift wrapping business perfectly. But also think in terms of longevity.

Things to Think About

Once you've decided on a name, you will need to file for a DBA (Doing Business As) with your local small business association (SBA). Visit sba.gov to learn more.

This is a great time to purchase your domain name and social media account names after making sure they aren't taken by someone else. This is an important step. Do your research! Once you have your name, search to see if it is available.

Next, you can take the proof of your new DBA to your local bank for an official business bank account. You will want to keep all personal and business banking separate. I also recommend a credit card that is only for business.

How to Set up a Dedicated Workspace

There's a big difference between the way you feel when you walk into an office at a traditional job and the way you feel when you walk into the gift wrapping studio you created yourself. One represents an environment where you have no control. The other is organized to your distinct specifications and in a manner that encourages joy and inspiration every time you walk through the door.

Let's unleash your creativity and apply it to setting up your unique gift wrapping business workspace—the place where magic happens.

Let's walk through structuring a well-appointed studio where your designing, product storage, and administration will occur.

Setting up your workspace is like announcing to yourself and the world that "I'm in business!" You have the credentials, which we discussed in a prior lesson. But you'll also soon organize the studio that will be home to your mobile gift wrapping business.

First, we'll choose a place to set up your studio. Next, we'll find a place for the items we identified earlier—which you might have in front of you now—so that everything is within reach, whether you're wrapping gifts or processing orders. Finally, we'll discuss a few extra ideas that you may want to consider incorporating.

Then we will work on how to transport everything when you are working on-site, which will be where you do most of your work.

It may be difficult right now to see how all of this will come together. Rest assured that when it's done, that same feeling of accomplishment you experience the first time you set up this new space will greet you every time you enter the studio

Choosing a Design Space

Have you heard stories about how entrepreneurs start businesses on kitchen tables? That's how it was for me! While these tales may be true, successful mobile gift wrappers quickly learn that moving from the kitchen table into a dedicated workplace is the only way to truly succeed. This is due to a variety of reasons.

Why You Need a Space for Your Business

1. State and county laws say that you must set up and maintain business in one place. There's very little chance that a regional representative will inspect your facility;

however, it's wise and in your best interest to be prepared and professional.

2. Although it's ideal to create a working area that's separate from your personal living space, that is not always possible. I use every area for my business. I have a cool mid-century desk in my living room and primarily work there. However, I live alone, so it works for me. I have a second office, where I have inspiration and handle all personal finance and investments. I also have my garage as a workspace, where crafting and wrapping happens and all my mobile supplies are at hand.

3. Surrounding yourself in a business-only environment helps tremendously and positively changes your frame of mind from wrapping gifts as a hobby to creating and wrapping for profit.

You may have started wrapping gifts on a kitchen table or your floor. Since you're sure that mobile gift wrapping is the right business for you, it's time to start searching for a place to call your design studio.

How to Set up a Dedicated Workspace in Your Home Business

Organizing your workspace at home combines convenience and cost savings. That is why I started Nifty Package Co. I wanted and needed the convenience of working for myself in an environment where I could still be available for my children who were still living at home after my husband passed away. Now they are out of the home and have been for many years. I have three shops, a very large storage, unit and two home offices, as well as garage space that serves as a craft or video space.

Three Reasons to Work from Home

1. There's no extra cost to maintain a separate brick-and-mortar store, which saves money you can use to buy supplies.

2. You will have the freedom to drive to your clients or pick up gifts, then drop them back off. But you are working for yourself.

3. When you're done for the day, you simply close the door of your space, the trunk of your car, or the door of your van and immediately reenter your residence.

Ready to set up your creative sanctuary? Let's transform an ordinary space into a studio brimming with joy, inspiration, and efficiency. It's your first big step in announcing to the world (and, more importantly, to yourself!) that you mean business.

Let's dive in and shape the place where your magical wrapping will come to life.

Step 1: Choose your design space

Finding the perfect spot for your studio is crucial. While the kitchen table might have been a great starting point, a dedicated workspace is key if you wish to truly thrive. Whether it's a cozy corner in your living room with a vintage desk, a spare room transformed into an oasis of creativity, or even a section of your garage dedicated to crafting and storing supplies, select a space that separates business from personal life. This not only boosts professionalism but also mentally shifts your approach from a hobby to a profit-driven craft.

Step 2: Set up your space

Once you've chosen your space, it's time to tailor it to your needs:

- **Organization:** Make sure everything you need is easily accessible. This includes materials for wrapping and processing orders, as well as any tools or supplies identified in later chapters.

- **Furniture:** A sturdy table or flat surface for wrapping gifts is a must. Consider ergonomics so you can keep your workflow smooth and comfortable.

- **Lighting:** Good lighting is not just for productivity. It's also crucial for photographing your beautifully wrapped gifts to showcase your work.

- **Inspiration area:** Set aside a space for inspiration and brainstorming. This could be a mood board or a corner with items that spark creativity.

- **Mobile prep:** Plan how you'll transport your supplies for on-site work. Organize your tools and materials so they are easily movable, ensuring you're always ready to bring your services directly to your clients.

- **Phone:** You might want to consider a landline phone with an 800 number. This part has been a challenge for me because I love the personal connection with my clients and potential clients. I like to know them, but the advantage is that it separates your personal phone from your business phone.

Organizing Your Space

Put everything in its place, but be able to carry everything in your car because you are mobile!

Have a checklist to make sure you have all the items you'll need. The *products* are the items you use to wrap the gifts, such as paper, ribbons, embellishments, boxes, and tissue. The *supplies* are the design tools you need, including scissors, tape, and a glue gun. The *equipment* is what keeps your space organized. So, let's review that list:

Equipment

- Worktable (six-foot fold-up with a handle so you can carry it with you on jobs)
- Ribbon rack or storage container
- Storage containers
- Storage shelves
- Mobile gift wrap carrier
- Glue gun
- Camera
- Computer
- Printer
- Accounting software
- Cell phone (you may also consider getting a landline)

I suggest that you not buy something if you can make do with what you have until you start creating income. Use a table you already have at the house, rely on your iPhone, utilize your old glue gun—whatever you might have. I suggest having three different types of scissors—one for ribbon, one for paper, and one for tape.

And it's helpful to label everything by color and season.

Everyone organizes a little differently, but when I started Nifty, I knew I wanted a large, successful business, so I started organizing that way.

My brand colors are pink, black, white, and eucalyptus, so my files are pink with black holders.

I have a nonprofit. Those files are yellow.

I am also an investor. Those files are gray.

Do you see the pattern? Don't get carried away by the office, but focus on the goal: to make money wrapping gifts for others to make a profit and be successful!

Make sure that you keep close everything you need to make a sale, organize your file, do on-site wrapping, or load information into your CRM (customer relationship management) software. I suggest doing a search for the best free CRMs or using a spreadsheet to track your contacts, conversations, and purchases. Simple is best! Copper can be set up with your Gmail account, is fairly inexpensive, and helps gather information that you otherwise would have to go get. This is an important step that can really help you if it's done correctly from the beginning.

The supplies you assemble will help determine who your clients will be. Do you want to use high-quality paper, ribbon, or tape? Or just use what you can buy at the local store or on Amazon?

Nifty can help you with all the best supplies, like what I use in my Mobile Gift Wrapping System in a Bag. It is full of your first holiday gift wrapping paper and all the supplies you need to go out on your first wrap job (except for the table).

Step 3: Involve your household

If you share your home, involve your family or housemates in the decision. Their support and understanding are key to harmoniously integrating your business space with your home life.

51

Step 4: Remember lighting and photography

Consider lighting not just for the work at hand but also for photographing your creations. Natural light is ideal, but if that's not possible, invest in good-quality artificial lighting to capture the true beauty of your work.

By carefully selecting and setting up your workspace, you're laying the foundation for a successful mobile gift wrapping business. Remember, this space is where you'll spend a lot of time creating, innovating, and growing your business. Make it a place that inspires you every day.

Build a Simple But Beautiful Website That Evokes "Like, Know, and Trust"

Marketing is the most important job you can do as an entrepreneur. And it's a lesson that took me a long time to learn. I want you to be successful, so let's discuss this in detail.

Marketing isn't just about your website. You are the marketer of a mobile gift wrapping business, which encompasses the calls you make, the website you build, the people you talk to for generating new leads, and the copy you use.

Before you even think about your website, you need to know who you are marketing to. This is very important. Not all clients are created equal. This is something that is probably neglected more than anything else in business. You need to know who your ideal client avatar (ICA) is. This is your ideal person who can and will purchase from you.

Understanding who you are selling to is a huge skill. Let me give you an example. McDonald's exists for parents or grandparents. The playplaces at McDonald's were awesome! Without going into details about how terrible the quality of the food is, McDonald's was still a place parents could take children to after school, on the weekends, in the rain, or in the heat. It was a place for those of us who needed something to do with children. McDonald's has removed most of the playplaces that were inside the fast-food chain, increased costs, and made the environment sterile. There are no longer sweet smiles or greetings. There are more computer check-ins, and now they are empty. McDonald's forgot who their clients are. Don't lose sight of who your clients are.

Many of us, as marketers, forget this important step. My clients or leads are not purchasing from Harry & David's or Wine Country Gift Baskets. Their purchases are more along the lines of Williams Sonoma. They are busy yet classy people who love design and perfection. They have limited time and value convenience. If people say they cannot afford your wrap, they are not your ideal client. I have my potential client all spelled out, including how they dress and the kind of car they drive. I gave you this exercise earlier.

You might especially need to work on your ideal potential client when you're starting out because you don't necessarily have clients yet. Know what your potential clients have going on in their heads. For example, if they want a gift basket, they might search for how to make a gift basket versus the word gift basket. They might type in a phrase like "gift wrapper near me." As you get to know your clients and leads better, you will want to make understanding what is going on in their heads a priority. Get to know who your potential clients are and do a deep dive into their emotions, careers, what keeps them up at night, and how you can serve them. You'll use this message in all your marketing materials, such as your website, Instagram, Pinterest, and LinkedIn.

Conclusion

Keep in mind that as you embrace your new mobile gift wrapping business or extension of a business, all these ideas—understanding your ideal client, choosing your business name, setting up a designated workspace, and disciplining your life—are important to the overall success right from the beginning.

3

Purchasing Products and Supplies to Get Started

As I was walking on the cobblestone streets in Florence, Italy, this past week, I admired the quality of the items sold, the buildings around me, and the handcrafted paper I saw in shop windows. The quality of a finished product starts with the items first used to construct it. The same applies to the quality and beauty of the paper, ribbon, and supplies you use. Your future clients will notice the quality of your ribbon and paper. In this chapter, I will discuss the types of supplies you need as you get started on your journey to become successful. Eventually, you'll be able to charge higher prices thanks to the overall value of your presentation.

Brown Paper Packages Wrapped up in String!

Let's talk paper.

Although you can get away with kraft paper—brown paper that looks like vintage wrapping and is very popular due to its ability to get dressed up for all occasions—I also use different unique colors, textures, and fabrics. I have all of these handy all the time. I do tend to pay full price for wrapping paper because I want the best for my family and my clients. Paper is such a beautiful way to elevate your gift wrapping. When it comes to the major supplies, paper, ribbon, and embellishments are where you splurge. I have spring colors, pastels, black, dark green, tan, pink, baby, Mother's Day wrap, and more. You name it, I have it.

Good-quality gift wrapping paper is a key element in creating a beautifully wrapped gift and is key for charging a premium price. When you're looking for high-quality gift wrapping paper, there are several factors to consider to ensure that you find the perfect one for your gifts. Here are some key characteristics to look for:

Durability: Good-quality gift wrapping paper should be durable and able to withstand the rigors of handling and shipping. Look for paper that is made from heavy-duty materials and is less likely to tear or rip.

Texture: Gift wrapping paper comes in a variety of textures, from smooth to textured. Textured papers can add an extra element of interest and help create a more unique and personalized look.

Color: Good-quality gift wrapping paper has vibrant and consistent colors that will not fade or run over time. Look for papers that are printed with high-quality inks that are resistant to fading and bleeding.

Finish: The finish of the paper can also affect its quality. Look for a smooth finish that will not scratch or snag easily. Also, you don't want paper with a dark front and light back because when you crease the corners, the color shows through and looks unprofessional.

Acid-free: Good-quality gift wrapping paper should be free of acids to ensure that it will not yellow or degrade over time. Acid-free paper is made from materials that are less likely to react with the inks and other materials used in it, ensuring that your gifts will look great for years to come.

Recyclable: Many consumers are looking for eco-friendly and sustainable gift wrapping options. Look for paper that is recyclable or made from recycled materials to reduce your environmental impact.

Overall, good-quality gift wrapping paper should be durable, have vibrant and consistent colors, have a smooth finish, be acid-free, and be recyclable. By considering these factors, you can find the perfect paper for your gifts and create a beautiful and memorable unboxing experience for your recipients.

Purchase Your Supplies

1. Ribbon

I use only fabric ribbons, such as satin, grosgrain, twine, cotton, silk, and others that are key for my designs. You'll collect many for their varied styles and colors. You can choose from a variety of other options, such as raffia and paper ribbon, but your use of them will depend on the client and the gift you are wrapping. Nifty did a gift wrap for Disney for the Oscars and had to use its logo ribbon. Unfortunately, it is not easy to work with and does not have the beauty that the others have.

- Store your ribbons efficiently to avoid clutter. Think of them as investments; choose wisely to prevent waste.

2. Wrapping paper

- Diverse materials (such as tulle, newsprint, and kraft paper) and colors are your palette. Mix, match, and stay current with trends.
- Organize and store samples for easy access and inspiration.

3. Camera

- Documenting your work with photos is essential for marketing because this is how you show your work. Pictures are everything in this business, and they're how I got my biggest clients. Make sure you take pictures of all sides and the top of a gift, along with different styles of the same layout. I still do not have a camera, but I use my iPhone for everything. You can use what you have. But consider choosing high resolution on your settings when you take pictures.

- If you have a digital camera, feel free to use it. You have a few options here, and you can use simple backgrounds (neutral wall, white sheet) to highlight your designs. I use an old wooden door or a white wooden table. My brand is vintage and modern mid-century, and these backgrounds fit my style. Yours might be a little different.

- Consistency in your photo style reflects your brand. Set aside a specific spot in your studio for shooting or use a few different places—but keep them consistent. When I started out, I did not understand how important this was, so I used a few different backgrounds and took terrible pictures. But it did not stop me from taking the pictures and posting them.

Efficiency Tips

- Keep a checklist for inventory needs.

- Remember to photograph each project for your portfolio and client records. They love the images themselves, and it helps you keep a copy for future references that can also be used on your social media accounts. Remember: If you have high-profile clients like I do, you have to get permission to post those images. But still take them.

The tips above ensure that you're prepared to create, present, and promote your gift wrapping business effectively and efficiently.

Keep Your Supplies Organized

I often use every part of my home, so learning to put everything away is important. But to be honest, it doesn't always happen. Since I am not married, I can keep some things out. Also, now I have shops and a storage unit, and my supplies are there. So I do go back and forth now, and I have to think through what I need to take or bring back.

When you know where everything is, you're able to tell someone where things are, you know the state of your business, and you have all your supplies ready to go at any moment. Also, once you've done your first mobile wrap, you will know what is missing or what you use the most. Take advantage of the supply list I give you in the course called Your Mobile Gift Wrapping Business Boss Class.

Your First Gift Wrap

We've been talking a lot about wrapped gifts, but let's take a quick look at how to actually wrap one. The basic products and tools needed to wrap a gift are a mix of familiar items (which you've seen in wrapped gifts in retail stores) and items you may not recognize. Before buying anything new, I encourage you to look at the following list and see what's available around your home. There's a good chance you won't have to buy many of the things that you may include in your first design.

Here's what you'll need:

- A small box (ten inches or less in diameter) of any shape. If you don't have one handy, you can use a shoe box.

- Your favorite gift wrap paper or brown kraft paper.
- Double-sided professional gift wrap tape.
- Ribbon, which is included in your kit.
- A gift tag.
- Fabric bows, which are the Nifty way (we do *not* use any other kind).

Gather all these items, then place them on a clean table. Guess what? You're now prepared for your first gift wrapping tutorial!

First, Get into the Gift Wrapping Mindset!

Now that you've gathered the supplies for your first professional gift wrap, you're ready to transform a box into a luxury gift you would want to receive. If you don't have your permanent design space set up yet, don't worry. My first gift wrap was done on a floor. It was a big mess when I finished, but I completed the steps and was proud of my accomplishments. You will be too! (Actually, I wrapped every gift, forgot to label them, and had to rewrap every gift! But I learned!)

Think of a certain person as you design this gift wrap. It may be a friend, relative, or coworker. Use the beautiful Nifty paper included in your kit (which you received if you signed up for the course), and think about why you're wrapping this gift. In just ten steps, this special gift will be ready to give to someone who really deserves it. Get a cup of your favorite tea or wonderful coffee, and let's begin!

We've seen how starting your own mobile gift wrapping business can combine your love of creating something beautiful with your hands and provide a healthy income that can take care of your financial needs. You can expect new and wonderful challenges every day because a mobile gift wrapper entrepreneur's life is much different than anything you may have experienced before. One day, you're up to your elbows in orders, and another day, you're meeting customers or delivering wrapped gifts you made the day before.

Most new mobile gift wrappers start their businesses at home, so be ready to spend time preparing part of a room or an entire space for this enterprise. Create a schedule to track when you'll wrap gifts and when you'll tend to family concerns. This is very important because your home is also the place where you design.

You can start wrapping gifts on a part-time basis or launch your business full-time, but remember not to quit your full-time job before you're up and running. It's up to you how much of your day you'll dedicate to creating a fulfilling business, and the decision will impact how much you earn in a week, a month, or a year.

It's a joy to welcome you into the mobile gift wrapping business world. I know you're eager to start, so let's move on. You'll learn more about gift wrapping designing and differentiating your style from others in the industry. You can find more details on this in the online mobile gift wrapping course.

Essential Tools and Materials

There are necessary tools and materials for mobile gift wrapping. My list for you is below.

Wrap Date & Time :

_____ / _____ / _____

Your Logo Here

Client Name:

Address:

Phone: Email:

S U P P L I E S   N E E D E D

- [ ] Table & Chairs
- [ ] Pink Tablecloth
- [ ] Table Toppers & Decos
- [ ] 8-10 ft Kraft Paper
- [ ] Blue Painter Tape
- [ ] Boxes
- [ ] Tissue Paper
- [ ] Wrapping Paper
- [ ] Scissors
- [ ] Ruler & Tape Measurer
- [ ] Double-Sided Scotch Tape
- [ ] Double-Sided Film Tape
- [ ] One-Sided Scotch Tape
- [ ] Glue Dots
- [ ] Clear Packing Tape
- [ ]

- [ ] Creasing Tool
- [ ] Ribbon
- [ ] Tulle
- [ ] Embellishments
- [ ] Gift Tags
- [ ] Order Tracking Tickets
- [ ] Pens
- [ ] Sharpies
- [ ] Post It Notes
- [ ] First Aid Kit
- [ ] Hand Cleaner
- [ ] Antibacterial Wipes
- [ ] Trash Bags
- [ ] Hand Broom/Vacuum
- [ ] Tip Jar
- [ ]

Notes:

YOUR COMPANY NAME HERE

You will need some space, a vehicle, and two or three pairs of scissors.

There are different types of wrapping papers, ribbons, bows, and embellishments. You might choose to use recycled paper, kraft, newspaper, and stunning wrapping paper. Although you want cost-effective options, you truly want to use the best-quality materials in your wraps. Your clients are paying you well for this.

You also want fabric ribbons, cotton, satin, and burlap. But don't use paper ribbons. If you are using the Nifty license, you cannot do so. Everyone who is a licensee should wrap well and professionally. That's how you can charge the premium price. If someone doesn't do it well, it affects all of us who wrap professionally.

You can find a template for your Mobile Gift Wrap Checklist here: michellemhensley.com/list

The most exciting part about starting a gift wrapping business is learning how to design the gift wrapping. It's important to know all about finances, competition, and marketing too. But that's not what attracts customers. They want to see beautifully wrapped gifts that make them say, "Wow." That's why we're going to take a closer look at gift wrap designs.

In this lesson, you'll master your design abilities and become confident in creating professionally wrapped gifts.

Here are three tips to keep in mind as you work through this:

1. **Go slowly:** Wrapping gifts is exciting, but be sure to follow all directions. Read them a second time if needed.

2. **Check all sides of the gift:** Does your technique look professional? Keep going when you're sure that your wrap is on the right track. I train wrappers to use a blind gift wrap. This is what will set you apart.

3. **Blind wrap image and non-blind wrap image:** A blind wrap is where you don't see the lines on the wrapping. That's why it is called a blind wrap. I am known for this wrap, and so is Nifty. It looks very clean and stunning. Most other people wrap without thinking about where the line is.

Gather Your Materials to Set up Shop

- ❏ INVENTORY
- ❏ Small supply pouch
- ❏ Gold-handled scissors (for paper and ribbon only)
- ❏ Standard scissors (for tape, when necessary)
- ❏ Glue sticks
- ❏ Post-it notes (3x3)
- ❏ Nifty Pink Post-it notes (3x3)
- ❏ Scoring tool (To help smooth out the edges of more complicated wraps; see picture)
- ❏ Tape measure
- ❏ Pens
- ❏ Extra-fine black Sharpies
- ❏ Black Sharpies
- ❏ Double-sided scotch tape (permanent)
- ❏ Single-sided scotch tape
- ❏ Double-sided film tape
- ❏ Small glue gun
- ❏ Numbered tickets with tear-off stub (These are important for keeping track of gifts and clients when you're in a store or client event. You want to get the information from the person who is having you wrap so you can label and put it with the gift. This keeps the gift and the name together. The ticket is a claim ticket for the gifts.)
- ❏ White collapsible gift boxes (8.5x11)
- ❏ Roll of half-inch light-pink velvet ribbon (at least 21 yards)
- ❏ Roll of half-inch black grosgrain ribbon (at least 21 yards)

❑ Nifty gift wrapping

❑ Glue dots

❑ Broom and dustpan

❑ Vacuum

4

Gift Wrapping Techniques

There is an art to gift wrapping. And that's one of the reasons you are hired—to make gifts beautiful and ready to be photographed!

This is where your personal style begins to take shape. You will learn what you like, how you wrap, and what colors are your signature style. Nifty's is a 1940s black-and-white look and feel. It's very modern vintage, yet beautiful. I love different color combinations. This is what you will be known for; however, your style will evolve based on the jobs you are hired to create and do. I have done very trendy, edgy wraps and love those, but they aren't necessarily my personal style.

It takes a while to find your style, so know that it will evolve and look like your creativity. I use only fabric ribbon, blind wraps, Japanese wraps, and some trendy, unique styles. For me, it depends on the client and recipient.

For example, I received a call from a client who needed a culturally wrapped gift for a Chinese hundred-day birthday celebration. The baby was a girl. This occasion represents the well-being of the baby and celebrates that the baby will live a hundred years. Gold and red are important colors for this type of celebration. My suggestion was to wrap the gift in white with red tulle and a little touch of gold.

In an age when we are becoming increasingly concerned about the environment, measuring paper (and ribbon) is key to avoiding waste. It will also save you money, so you will want to use up those remnants and roll ends so nothing goes to waste. At Nifty, I save my ribbons and press them later for another gift. I am very big on saving scraps!

For some video training, check out our gift wrapping tutorials! https://www.youtube.com/@mobilegiftwrapbusinesscoach/featured

You can easily find colors you like and start watching gift wrapping videos. YouTube has so many valuable ones.

The blind wrap is one of our main and most important wraps, and I highly recommend it. I teach it in the mobile gift wrapping course.

If you are wrapping on-site for a client like a family, use color-coordinated paper and ribbon. It looks great and makes it easy for the client to see which gift belongs to which recipient.

Sometimes, the client has paper, so part of my discussion ahead of time is, "Do you have paper already you love and want to use or am I good to bring my paper, and if bringing my paper, do you like traditional wrap, gold and silvers, rustic, nontraditional . . ." I get a feel for their style and bring those.

Practice

Practice makes you a better and more professional gift wrapper. But trust me, all of us pros still mess up paper and ribbon. The rule of thumb is to measure twice, cut once.

How do you practice wrapping and get good at it?

Creating beautifully wrapped gifts is such a wonderful way to express your creativity and impress your loved ones and clients with your newfound skills. The goal of this lesson is to prepare to wrap like a pro and acquire the skills you need to master wrapping a box and tying a beautiful bow.

It's so much easier to wrap a box with paper that's measured correctly, so keep in mind:

The importance of positioning your paper so you get a hidden seam

How easy it is to wrap without looking and maintaining a good posture

How you'll always want to use double-sided tape

Let me break out the steps:

Wrapping a Gift

Measure the Paper

You first want to measure your paper.

In this business, you are going to wrap a lot of boxes. So measuring right is key. Although this is a challenge we all face, getting better at measuring will save you money and time! Remember, measure twice, cut once. Sometimes you don't have a lot of paper left. I ran into this with a Justin and Hailey Bieber job. I had wrapped almost all their gifts and was getting very short on the paper for this custom wrap. I had to measure everything very well!

You can purchase many things already boxed, so it's good to know how to wrap a box perfectly and correctly calculate how much paper you'll need.

Since we are all becoming increasingly aware of the environment, it's ideal to measure paper (and ribbon) correctly in order to avoid waste.

This is when you actually learn to be a hoarder because a majority of the leftover materials can be stored and reused!

You will find that wrapping a box is so much easier when you use less paper. After some practice, you'll be able to measure by sight. It is key that you not have too much paper overlapping and that the sides of the box are measured correctly to avoid any bulky folding.

So grab a box, your scissors, and your wrap. Then, let's get measuring! No tape measure is required either.

First things first: Gift boxes are popular. And even if you're just using a small cardboard box as an alternative, you can make it instantly more luxurious if you line it with tissue. The item becomes far more elevated as a gift when you add tissue paper versus scrunching tissue inside a box! You don't always have to do this, but consider it.

I have worked with Van Cleef & Arpels, Mont Blanc, and Graff jewelers, and all of their purchases are beautifully boxed in this way. Even if you're wrapping a small, inexpensive gift in a cardboard box, you can use a few clever tricks to showcase it beautifully.

So grab a gift box and empty your table, as you'll need some space for this project.

Supplies for this example:

> Two pairs of scissors—one for cutting the paper and the other for tape (if you cut it)
>
> Double-sided tape, which you can purchase from me
>
> Permanent double-sided scotch tape
>
> Paper of your choice
>
> Ribbon to finish it!

Don't seal the paper until you make sure that both sides match. A quick way to check is to fold over the paper to make sure both sides are even, then make a small crease so both sides look the same. You don't always have to use a ruler, but I do. You want to make sure you have enough paper to go around the gift on all sides. You will want to check the ends of the gift box to make sure they are a little over half the height so you can close them nicely.

Place the correct side (wrong side of paper) facing up, and make sure you line up the gift properly.

Measure and cut the additional sides, like in this image. If you want to be a true professional, this is Nifty's blind wrap.

Gauge right up next to the edge, but *don't* tape yet. Just get the first side aligned.

Put the other end under this piece. This is so you will have the blind wrap edge once the first side is done. Now, tape the edge of the piece that will be under the blind wrap.

Place the small piece of double-sided scotch tape along the edge of only the length of the box. Place it securely on the edge.

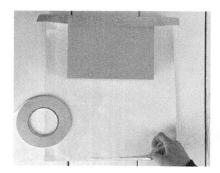 

Bring it all together.

You can't see the edge once you turn the gift all around.

Next, close the ends of both sides of the paper of the gift to finish it.

Make sure the edges, or point, depending on if it is a square box or rectangular or the look you are going for, are down or pointing down (see next image). Don't press the ends until you know you have enough for each side. Gauge both sides. Sometimes you don't have enough for one side. So, before pressing the edge, just confirm that both sides are pretty even, then press.

 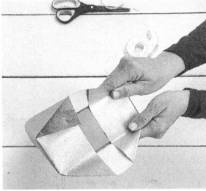

Finish up both sides, and make sure they are as even as you can get them.

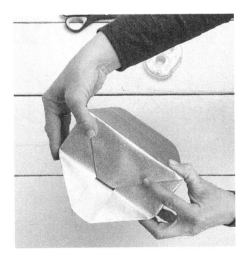

Make sure to make both sides even before the final taping.

Tuck in both sides to finish it.

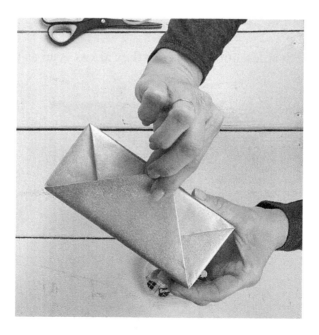

This end should be facing down. The blind wrap is also on the bottom.

Tape so all edges are clean. This is our double-sided gift wrapping tape.

Fold down for a smooth, professional look and finish to the gift.

Things to Keep in Mind

For many people, wrapping a box is an easy option. I often hear this view expressed in my gift wrapping courses. The key to getting this right is to measure your paper first, get the positioning right, ensure the paper is tight around the box, and use double-sided tape.

If you have too much excess paper, you will struggle to wrap the box, and the sides will become bulky. You will wrap thousands of boxes in your lifetime, so it's an important skill to measure the paper first and crease as you go along to make it more manageable.

My gift wrapping team members have to wrap from start to finish, including ribbon, within four to six minutes. With a bit of practice, you will become fast at wrapping too.

Once you've mastered the technique, you should be able to wrap with your eyes shut. Kind of!

Ribboning

Here are some images that show how to tie a beautiful ribbon.

You'll need to develop your skill of measuring the ribbon. The technique depends on the type of bow you're making

There are several types of ribbon, including the Tiffany bow, which is named after Tiffany's, the famous jewelry store. Here, I show you how to make this four-loop bow.

Measure the ribbon before cutting it. I like to have a flat back. This is the best and most professional look.

Cross over on both sides, and tie in the middle before you finalize the cut to make sure you have enough ribbon. Remember: measure twice, cut once.

Make the first loop.

Bring up the second loop to wrap around the first one.

Most of the time, you have to work with the bow to make it perfect!

Trim the edges for a beautiful finish.

There is a lot of pressure when you are on-site with clients. They sometimes stand there watching you. It's like when you have a plumber come over, and you hover over them. So when you are prepared, it is much easier to wrap when they happen to be there. Just know that your goal is threefold: you want five-star reviews, you want to serve and bring them joy, and you want to be paid!

I was worried about being perfect when I started because I charged higher prices. But I found that I just got better with every single wrap. Make sure you look at all sides of the wrap before you ribbon, trim, and embellish. Then hand over the gift. When you're out in the field, time is the issue, not perfection.

Don't be afraid to wrap outside the box. Meaning, be creative.

My preference is less is more. I'm not into huge toppers (embellishments) like big plastic plants or big wired bows. I prefer simple and elegant but unique and real, like a touch of lavender, eucalyptus, or dried oranges.

I create looks and feels based on the person, brand, or company. I also just create looks based on a style or the current popular Pantone colors. For example, I created a look and feel for the international dress styles of the 1940s using Simplicity dress patterns as guides.

Questions and Answers

Q: Why do we do the blind wrap?

A: This gift wrapping technique is by far the cleanest and most professional as a look and minimizes any mistakes. Every gift is consistent, so the client will love and appreciate the final wrapped product.

Q: Why only fabric ribbon?

A: For a few reasons. One, the way it looks is far superior and far more luxurious. It's also cleaner. Plus, it does not fade, so the recipient can save it. It is also a culturally accepted and well-received practice.

Q: Can I choose multicolor ribbons for gifts?

A: Absolutely. But this takes more time when you are out in the field. Since time equals money for the client, I suggest that you learn to wrap well with one ribbon and have a few embellishments that are easy to add after the fact if you have the time.

Q: Why is it important to spend as little time as possible when at a client's location?

A: Gift wrapping is fun and inventive, but learning to be good and fast increases your profits and is respectful of your clients. After all, they are paying a premium for your service. If you wrap only one gift in forty-five minutes and they are paying you $150, that does not bring them value at all. As you wrap more, you will soon master this. But I can wrap six to eight very professional and beautiful gifts per hour. Make sure you stay on top of your time. I do not start the clock until all my supplies are set up at the site and I am ready to wrap.

You know the saying: practice makes perfect! Well, it's true. The best way to become a better, faster designer is to practice, practice, practice.

At this point, you should have the materials for two gifts. Time yourself. See how long it takes you to wrap and ribbon. Now, do it a second time.

Unleashing Creativity with Mobile Gift Wrapping

As mentioned earlier, there are a few unique and more advanced gift wrapping techniques. Check out our YouTube for some ideas! Don't be afraid to wrap outside the box! Study your new craft!

I have wrapped for the UN, creating a unique design based on their color scheme. Understand the purpose of the gifting program, like we did for Too Faced Cosmetics:

You can personalize and brand around the company's theme. For example, what is the purpose of the gift or activation? (Activation means they are hiring you to be at their site or at a different location, like at a public event.)

Are you excited?

4

Growing Your Mobile Gift Wrapping Business

All this is great, but how do you start your own gift wrapping business, manage it, and create a profit?

As I mentioned before, you definitely need to have the desire and the skills of a professional gift wrapper, as described in the earlier chapters.

First, think about who you want to sell to! Write a description of your typical client. Think about the person's gender (man or woman), marital status, age range, home life, and extracurricular activities (such as sports, parties, and travels). This assignment will help you focus on the people you'll look for when you're ready to market, and it will give you ideas about how and where you'll find them. It will also help you determine the types of foods and gifts that your customer will want most.

Now you know you love to wrap and are just about ready to set up your business.

Next, let's think about the wrapped gift you made in the previous chapter.

P.S. Congrats on making it this far, blah blah blah. As a special gift to you, you get a coupon for the course. See the back of the book.

In the book, there is a coupon for an hour with me as well as a discount for the online course so you can start your own mobile gift wrapping business.

Time Is Money

How long did it take you to wrap this gift? Chances are you spent around forty-five minutes making sure that each step was properly done. Your design styling will get better and better, and you'll be able to wrap gifts faster and faster. As you become familiar with the process of wrapping gifts, your design time will decrease to ten to fifteen minutes, and that's good news.

Think of it this way. Let's say you are hired to wrap for two hours at $175 per hour with a two-hour minimum, and you wrap fifteen gifts. After supplies and your hourly rate, that will give you about $100 profit. Less time designing equals more per-minute profit. The design is still a masterpiece because your experience cuts out any guesswork that was once part of the process. As you do more, you get better and quicker.

Let me say this again: as you do more, you get better at your craft.

You might enjoy wrapping gifts, but remember that this is a business where you want to be as profitable as possible. The less time it takes you to wrap each gift, the more money you'll make. As you decrease your design time, the money you make for each minute of designing increases. That's the reason longtime professional gift wrappers search for ways to cut down their design time. It's also how they earn high daily revenue.

Gift wrapping takes time to learn, and there are huge benefits as you master your design style. It's important to go slowly at first, building your confidence and understanding of each step, from choosing the paper to adding the bow.

Whenever you wrap a gift, be sure to have your supplies ready and arranged on a clean tabletop with lots of space.

Best of all, you now know the basics of the art of gift wrapping and can create beautiful gifts for every event and occasion.

Pricing

Let's start with determining pricing before you head out on your first wrap!

Pricing is important for a variety of reasons. You are in business to make a profit and grow. Although you may have a different original reason, we have to be realistic about making a profit.

It's important to point out that your initial sales won't immediately pay your business start-up costs. When you get started, you'll buy a lot of inventory and supplies, which are necessary to begin this business. However, with the help of your marketing plan, social media marketing, and website, you will eventually become known for what you do and the services you provide. Then your business will grow.

Figuring out how much to charge a client is easier than you may imagine because you will have predetermined prices. The price will be determined by how much you pay for all the components that make up the design, plus an additional amount known as markup. The markup is the amount added to the cost of an item to determine its selling price.

You have to charge a client more than the cost of inventory and labor, or you'll quickly be out of business. Every retail business marks up their prices to earn revenue. That's also your mission.

What Determines Your Gift Wrapping Price?

You're on the right track if you think that the cost of everything added to a gift wrap job determines what you should charge for it. But that's just the beginning. You'll need to consider four types of business costs when you determine prices.

1. **Gift wrapping supplies:** You already understand these costs. You pay wholesale for gift wrapping products, and you recover those costs through the retail price you charge each client.

2. **Markup charge:** You'll determine a price for each client to pay over and above the wholesale costs. The markup is also referred to as a labor charge.

3. **Shipping charges:** When a wholesaler ships gift wrapping supplies from their facility to your design studio, they add a shipping charge. How do you incorporate that cost into your gift wrapping price? You split the charge evenly into the cost of each gift.

   For example, if you purchase five spools of ribbon for $7.50, for a total of $37.50, and the shipping charge amounts to $10, the cost for each of the spools increases by $2 ($10 divided by 5 equals $2). Each ribbon spool now costs $9.50 ($7.50 plus $2 equals $9.50).

4. **Travel expenses and workspace:** Travel expenses—such as attending networking meetings, delivering wrapped gifts, and visiting stores to purchase gift wrap supplies— are necessary from time to time. Don't forget to include those costs when you determine price. I have four spaces I am responsible for, so all those costs are added to the price

for the client. Since you are working from home, electricity and other costs need to be accounted for.

What about expenses for the area where you wrap gift baskets? It's easy to overlook your workspace, but it's necessary and wise to incorporate these costs into the price.

How do you do that? First, you list all the administrative expenses that keep your business running smoothly. Then, you separate those expenses into two categories: fixed and variable.

Fixed Costs and Variable Costs

A fixed cost is an expense that arrives each month without fail. A variable cost changes from month to month. Utilities, such as gas and electricity, are fixed costs. Unless you have a standing appointment to visit a customer or pick up products every month, vehicle mileage is a variable cost. It's usually labeled as variable because there will be times when you travel many miles for business and other times when travel won't be as extensive. Variable costs are also the category for one-time purchases, such as when you buy a computer or printer.

Your start-up costs might be covered in the first year. However, you most likely will be able to recover your costs in the second year and make a profit.

Keep in mind who your client is. They are someone who does not have the time to wrap gifts but loves the idea of you doing that work for them so the wrapped gifts look amazing for their holiday, their board of directors, or whatever you might be wrapping for. Your prices need to reflect this.

If you wrap one gift depending on size, that is setting aside a half hour of time. So, the gift wrap should cover your labor and cost of goods (which is what it is called).

There are on-site prices and in-house pricing.

The main difference between the two is the cost of pickup and delivery. If you are at the customer's location, you primarily charge hourly. Sometimes you are at their location and wrapping the same gifts over and over. If that is the case, I charge per gift wrapped. I always encourage the client to send me pictures of the gift and the measurements because what they think is small might actually be medium. You will learn this throughout the start of your business.

Hourly Rate

Set an hourly rate starting with a base of $75 to $100 per hour. You can increase your prices as you grow in your craft and your clients. If you are traveling to the client, you should also charge a travel fee.

I charge a travel fee to pick up and deliver to help cover gas and mileage. This is a flat rate. When I have a drive that is over an hour, I charge $150. I put this on a separate line for costs so I can separate the costs for the client to see.

Per-Project Rate

This is a set flat rate for the entire gift wrapping project per gift. You can base the fee on the total number of gifts you are to wrap, the paper, the fabric, the ribbon, and possibly the boxes. Include shipping boxes if you are shipping back or delivering. You must take all of these factors into account. The charge also will depend on how fast you work, whether you have a team, and how accurate you are. The more practiced and accurate you are, the more gifts you'll be able to wrap in a single sitting. A suggested rule of thumb can be:

Five to ten small gifts are $25 to $5 per wrap, depending on how much time you think it will take to complete.

A simpler wrap will take less time. If it's more complicated, charge on the higher end of the range.

For example, if you have five gifts that are fairly simple and can be completed in ninety minutes, a good estimate is 5 x $25, or $125.

It's always a good idea to err on the side of caution and charge a bit more than you think; most wraps are not as simple as they seem. A more conservative estimate would be 5 x $40, or $200.

If you have a high-volume project, you can negotiate the price down. So, if you are wrapping four hundred gifts, you can charge $23 per gift because all your costs for the supplies will be down. However, the labor costs do not go down, so you must keep this in mind.

Platforms and Resources

I highly recommend an accounting program. Probably the best is QuickBooks Online. I use QuickBooks Desktop because that is what I started with. Plus, my bookkeeper and accountant use it as well. I suggest that you research your options and find out what fees are involved. Also look into how to deposit funds into your account, how to make online purchases, and what their customer support is like. Make sure you read the reviews.

You will also want to research and choose an online payment platform and credit card reader. There are so many great ways to collect money from your clients, but the most important way will be through your website and its POS (point of sale) system. If you choose to launch on Shopify, you can use their reader. This is so you can process payments in person.

Your bank may also have a reader or POS.

You can collect from QuickBooks, Venmo, Zelle with your online banking, Stripe, PayPal, and others. Look out for the hidden fees and charges. These change regularly, unfortunately, so you need to keep an eye out. I want to make it easy for my clients, so I take all and any forms of payment.

You can keep an eye out for your daily earnings, online payments, reissued receipts, and more via these platforms. Most readers are easy to set up. After linking your business checking account to it, most payments are deposited the next business day.

Here is a list of a few credit card readers to select from:

PayPal

Venmo

Clover

With most online payment platforms, deposits are made on the very next business day.

Tipping

I recommend not having a tip jar. The US is overwhelmed with tipping, and if the client feels up to it, trust me—they will tip you. I have received gift cards and $100 cash tips. So has the team, and it always brings joy. Reducing their stress and delivering what they need is a blessing to the client. If they feel moved, they will tip. But do not ever expect or ask for it.

This Little Gifter
Went to Market

All things marketing!

At this point, I discuss building a simple but beautiful website that evokes "like, know, and trust." So, we will focus now on the other parts of marketing your mobile gift wrapping business. This includes:

- Digital marketing: Social media, newsletters, permission-based marketing, and the new anti-spam laws

- In-person marketing: Meetups, outreach, networking, and pay-to-play ideas to get new customers (i.e., Balboa Bay Club)

If marketing is number one in this area, your lead/client list is number two.

Opportunities to let customers know about your mobile gift wrapping business are all around you. Which will you choose?

First, we'll cover the difference between marketing and advertising. Next, we'll look at marketing techniques, from business cards to online marketing campaigns. You can spend a lot of money promoting your business, but the good news is you don't have to. If you took the mini course, you already have an idea of what you want to do, but this is very important. Wrapping gifts is one thing, but growing your mobile gift wrapping business is another.

Let's get started!

Rule Number One

Never go somewhere to meet someone new or attend an event around your marketing or networking without a wrapped gift! This always starts a conversation. Because a mobile gift wrapping business is unique and a very new concept, this opens up dialog about how people love beautiful gifts but do not like wrapping. Or, maybe they love wrapping gifts, and the topic is fun!

The goal here is to spread the word about what you do. Ideally, it would be nice to have all your social media accounts and website set up, but I didn't do that before I went to my first chamber of commerce meeting. I just showed up with gifts, and there it started!

When I attend any meeting, I show up with a black basket (which is our look) full of goodies! I give very professional (my best paper) little pink or tan boxes of fair trade chocolate, my contact information, and a brochure about what we do. That gives the client an idea of our professional wrap and a little treat with all my contact information in it.

Rule Number Two

Create a business card and a gift card that creates a picture of what you do, including all your information, and keep some in your purse at all times. Right now, while finishing this book, I am at an exceptional marketing conference. I use both a traditional business card and a gift card. This small but powerful card tells what I do and who I am, is a call to action (CTA), and offers a discount and several ways to reach me.

Here's a sample:

Spring has Sprung!

As this lovely season unfolds, we're happy to
reveal our newest collection of gifts.
Our incredible baskets for caregivers, medical
professionals and moms are thoughtfully
curated to show love and gratitude for these
special folks.

Place a gift basket order OR refer a friend before
June 21 and receive 10% off.

Michelle
& the Nifty Team!

Rule Number Three

As you start out and even after your business is up and running, some things are just going to cost you money because, as an entrepreneur, you will be putting things out there before you actually sell. This is important because of the spirit of reciprocity. I am known as the basket lady. My future and current clients know or remember that I bring cool little gifts in a basket to give away. I tend to have a gift giveaway at events. You are remembered because of that. If you send off a small gift similar to what I described, many (not all, but some) will want to give back. This technique creates an experience with you, the mobile gift wrapper.

Marketing Your Exciting Mobile Gift Wrapping Business

There is a lot of information out there on marketing, but just going out and starting a conversation is the best way to begin. From there, you will get fun conversations going. Many people are fascinated by the concept of mobile gift wrapping, whether they use your services or not and whether you drive to them or they come to you.

Word of Mouth and Referrals

This doesn't necessarily mean you will succeed just by word of mouth, but this can help grow your business. Getting five stars and glowing reviews is a way for people to tell others about what you do. This is how we got Justin and Hailey Bieber. Kendall Jenner told them what a great job we do and how she loves our team. This is important because it will spread the word, especially among celebrities and influencers.

Postcards and Direct Mail

Postcards are very important. So are small one-page or two-page images of what you have done. This is why you should keep taking pictures to show what you can do. Plus, you can reference them later and continue to perfect them. I suggest making this part of your strategy for growing your business. Postcards, letters, and note cards are also huge. There is a 98 percent open rate on postcards and handwritten letters. The copy (the written words on the postcard, website, and newsletters) and the images lead the potential client to what you can do for them.

A postcard can and probably will be saved. One idea is to have postcards made for each season. I have twelve and continue to build my postcard file. You can make these on Canva. They now print as well, or you can print them out at Staples or a local printer. They are less expensive to mail and well worth the cost.

There are several postcard manufacturers. Just do a Google or Bing search.

Digital Marketing

Flyers and newsletters are a great way to go. Some people will boo-hoo this, but don't listen. Write out stories and small lessons in the gift wrapping space, trends in color, trends in wrap, or cool wraps—especially as you start building your client and lead generation list. Most people have little time to read. But people are more likely to look at something that lands in their mailbox versus their inbox, especially when it includes images of gifts you have wrapped. It can also easily provide references to different news related to gift wrapping and your service. I have a Google Alert set to news about gift wrapping from around the world, which helps a lot when it comes to informing people about gift wrapping and trends.

Email newsletters are a great way to share some of your personal stories and link back to your gift wrapping business. People love stories and pictures. Both tell a lot! Keep in mind that there are new anti-spamming laws that mean you now have to have your leads and clients opt in to receive an email newsletter. This is why printed newsletters work very well. People are inundated with email. The volume is overwhelming, and your email might get lost in the process. I always ask for mailing addresses and grow my list.

Your list of potential clients is huge. This should be your main focus—grow your email and mailing lists so that you constantly have someone to reach out to and a way to keep track of your potential and current clients.

A small catalog of pictures is something to keep in mind for the future. You should be taking lots of photos of your gift wrapping. I recommend not overembellishing. Clean, attractive, meaningful wrap is best.

There are a lot of different methods available to market the gift wrapping you love to design. The challenge is picking from those ideas. Plus, most of the time, you don't know who to market to, or how. That's where we begin.

You get confused about where to start. Then you do nothing, which is an unfortunate disservice to the people who are ready and willing to buy your gift wrapping services. As Zig Ziglar famously said in a video from my memory, "My money is in their pockets and I have what they need."

You now have in your hands what it takes to be successful. With these creative and simple ideas, you'll be able to easily select the marketing options that are right for you right now.

I learned these techniques through decades of experimentation. When I began my gift basket business, I tried selling at pop-ups, gave away samples at chamber meetings, and met with corporations that let vendors sell products to staff. It took lots of time to prepare for those events. I lost money, and sales were slim to none. However, in my mind, most start this way. I learned what didn't work, which helped me think clearly about what might work better.

Word of mouth that I had started a gift basket business was my first form of marketing. Then I had to get creative. But I took the advice of other businesses. Even though I was terrified, I joined two local chamber of commerce locations and the Visit Anaheim MPI (Meeting Professionals International) group so I could get my name out there and grow comfortable speaking in front of others.

Although this was costly, it paid off over time. I was terrified to speak, had no idea what a business pitch was or how to say it, and didn't know what I should say. I just did it. I was also very big on what is called "lumpy mail." That's mail that is lumpy. I would send handwritten thank-you cards. I didn't use a service that prints on a note and sends it out for you. Do you know that 98 percent of handwritten letters get opened? Email, not so much. Then, I started giving away gift baskets and set up gifts on a table so people could see my work. And that is how I started the gift basket side.

Today, you and I have many more opportunities to succeed online, in print, in person, and through podcasts. This guide shares with you marketing ideas from my successes and the successes of designers all over the world who know how to make money and sell every day.

What you're about to learn won't cost much. What it will cost, in most cases, is time. So, be ready to take action on the ideas you know you can implement to be the success you want to be.

Forty Easy Ways to Market

Choose five to seven methods that you can use immediately. Remember that not everything is achievable quickly. The way to feel a sense of accomplishment is to focus on those tips that are easiest to do first. Then, at a later time, pursue others in this guide that take more effort to complete.

Resist thoughts of giving away your gift wrapping services just to get sales. You're here to create cash flow in a business, not a *free* business. I learned this the hard way. There are better ways to get orders. This guide provides smart choices to earn additional income.

Keep an open mind about direct mail. Yes, postage costs money. However, mailing your marketing materials also makes money because some people remember offers received by mail longer than they recall online promotions. This is, by far, one of the best ways to increase your mobile gift wrapping business.

I know you're ready, so let's get started.

1. Describe your business in a way that expresses how gift wrapping increases sales (if the person is a business owner), makes a big and positive impression (if the person is celebrating a special event such as a birthday or new baby), or saves time (no one wants to go from store to store when ordering from you is easier).

   If you simply say, "I wrap gifts," the potential client won't recognize the benefits of buying from you. State a phrase that solves a problem or meets a need, such as, "I help small businesses or million-dollar businesses make an incredible presentation of their gifts, therefore creating greater value that will help yours as well." That description encourages people to use my services.

2. Tailor your business card to include more than your name, telephone number, and website URL. Let them know you wrap gifts. Tell them that you are the mobile gift wrapper. Have wrap, will travel!

   Business cards are mini billboards that enhance promotions when they have information about your specialty, corporate expertise, customer comments, or other sales motivators printed on the front or back.

3. Choose and register your social media account name as soon as possible, even if you're not ready to begin marketing.

   Capturing your business name on Twitter, Facebook, Instagram, LinkedIn, YouTube, TikTok, and other social media platforms is an important brand identity strategy.

This is key. You do not want to be disappointed if someone else registers your business name to keep you from marketing your brand.

4. Display your beautifully wrapped gifts in places where prospective clients visit. This includes salons, mailbox centers, banks, and other locations where services are performed and where your prospects often travel. This also helps you get out in the community. Create spring looks, different wrapping, and Christmas-in-July looks. Nifty usually sets a tone for creative looks. You can look at our website to see some of what we have done.

   These are locations where you already have a relationship with the manager, representative, or business owner who approves a display that includes your business cards, wrapped boxes, brochures, or other information on your services.

   This may seem like an old-school marketing method. However, the more your wrapped gifts are seen, the more they create a reminder, make your phone ring, add orders to your online cart, and bring sales in other forms.

5. Select appropriate colors to introduce and reinforce your marketing campaigns. Certain colors are too bright or soft for some eyes to detect. I am very big on using trends and setting trends in colors. For example, several gifts wrapped in black and white are stunning. Other options are dark red on white, or silver on white. You can get a lot of ideas just by visiting the Nifty gift wrapping gallery, Pinterest, or our Instagram.

   I watch what the Pantone color of the year is, sign up for different gift wrap paper sites, and keep my eyes out for cool ideas. Color choices are an important consideration as you create or revise your logo, website, blog, social media accounts, and overall brand identity. But gift wrapping color ideas can be changed and reworked. Every holiday, we have a new collection of gift wrapping ideas and looks.

6. Ask family members and friends to support your business by recommending you to people they know in the work environment, networking groups, and houses of worship.

I heard a great statement on Instagram by Alex Hormozi: "The best gift a family member and friend can give to an entrepreneur is to order something, pay full price, and leave a great review."[6] Be careful and wise with your finances so you don't go overboard in giving things away. You need to earn income, as both groups often request discounts that end up costing you money. This well-known fact is why it may be better to ask them to refer you to their own contacts rather than ask friends and family to purchase from you. If their referrals place orders, consider how you will show appreciation for such support.

7. Organize a section in your car or other business vehicle to include postcards, business cards, and brochures for distribution wherever you travel. I keep some in my purse, including smaller postcards.

This way, you'll never be caught off-guard when you're on the road and asked for information. Consider the glove compartment, a back seat pocket, or the trunk as your mobile office.

8. Place a custom-made magnetic sign advertising your gift baskets on your vehicle in a place where drivers and passersby will see the message.

[6] Alex Hormozi (@username), "The best gift a family member and friend can give . . .," Instagram post, DATE, URL.

The most common areas for sign placement are on the driver's door, on the front passenger door, and (in the form of a decal) on the rear window.

9. Welcome incoming politicians (your town's mayor, council members, state or federal senator, assembly members, etc.) or incumbents celebrating an event with a small marketing gift wrapped beautifully to show all that you can do with gift wrapping.

   Don't be afraid to have someone take a photograph of you, the politician, and the wrapped gift, then put the image on your LinkedIn profile. You can include these photographs on your Facebook page and social media accounts as well.

   Each photo acts as a natural endorsement of your company.

10. Send an email with your well-put-together brochure—which you can make on Canva as an inexpensive platform for your gift wrapping sample photos—to prospective clients who have viewed your gift wrapping in person.

11. Specialize in at least four or five types of gift wrapping themes. Choose spring, Valentine's Day, red and white, black and white, silver or gray, birthday, corporate-branded wrap, or another occasion that sells fast and that customers associate with your business so you can start to create business all year long.

    Invest in a beautifully styled logo for image representation. Have the logo made by a professional artist in your local area or through a trusted online source suggested in the online Start Your Own Mobile Gift Wrapping Business course at michellemhensley.com.

    Make sure your logo request includes color and black-and-white options, as well as the ability to add the logo to every type of marketing material, such as business cards, tote bags, billboards, and your website.

12. Add twenty-dollar, thirty-five-dollar, and forty-dollar gift wrap ideas to your roster of designs. Include each one on your website, and talk about these options during networking events. Also, create unusual designs, such as fabric wraps, branding wrapping, and holiday sets.

    Individual clients will start to come once they know you wrap and find out that you will drive to them. Although retail sales did fairly well this year, many malls are closing, so your potential clients will be interested in convenience.

13. Keep your business's Facebook page updated and inspiring by planning what you'll promote each month. Ideas include contests, questions, and surveys; gift-giving success stories with a link to the longer story on your website or blog; and links to subscribe to your newsletter, YouTube channel, or another medium.

    Facebook allows you to add your website page as a tab on your company's Facebook page. Research this option and follow directions to include it.

14. Find podcasts and weekend television segments that will interview you about your business, the products you offer, or another topic that fits the season or show's description. These two promotional opportunities increase your social proof.

15. Get to know your clients; learn about their families, personal lives, and, pets when speaking with them during or after the sale. Such an inquiry is a good way to show concern and create new order opportunities. It proves to clients that their personal lives are just as important to you as their orders are.

    Make sure you are genuine. If you're not comfortable asking about family, inquire about something you prefer to discuss, such as golf, travel, or a client's profession. Or talk a little about how you started your business and why. That sometimes opens up dialogue.

Showing genuine concern encourages clients to continue buying from you and refer others to you.

16. Decide what you will send to clients as an appreciation gift before the end-of-year holidays arrive or at another time of your choosing.

    Gifting doesn't only occur in December. There will be times when you'll present customers with a gift if their orders or referrals have exceeded your internal goals.

    When you send a thank-you, lumpy mail, or a client-nurturing gift, make sure your brand stands out. I use pink or black puffy mailer. For different holidays and themes, I find creative ways to send fairly inexpensive gifts. For Christmas in November, I sent cute cards with a discount and pink-and-white or black-and-white candy canes. I do this about two to three times a year. Then I send Valentines as a great follow-up thank-you to the holiday clients and my other clients so they know Nifty loves them! I put in vintage Valentine cards, Sweethearts candies, and a discount card.

    Consider trendier, cooler items that make you stand out from competitors. Also, knowing your clients' preferences will help you select a curated gift that's highly appreciated.

17. Write editorial responses to magazines, newspapers, and online publications when luxury gifts are the featured story in print or broadcast.

    Readers are interested in the opinions of other readers, especially if those opinions disagree with the content or offer an alternative view about the topic.

    Your feedback will make more people aware of your name, your business and expertise, your website URL, and other details, which are hopefully printed with your comment.

18. Offer branded ribbon as part of your services. Many wholesale ribbon suppliers offer ribbon personalization, or you can invest in a machine that customizes ribbon. I brand the colors of the ribbon for the client because we don't always have the time to order the ribbon. Clients tend to want logo ribbon and order at the last minute.

   This service is invaluable when marketing gift wrapping to corporations that want to differentiate their brand from others when sending gifts to their investors or clients.

19. Contact clients as often as possible about new and current designs they may not know about. You can send postcards every month or quarter, publish a weekly online blog post, record a monthly podcast about gift giving, or participate in area charity events.

   Decide how to proceed and how much to spend within your budget. Create your action plan, and be proactive with organizing, distributing, and following up.

20. Allow your cell phone camera to document marketing ideas wherever you travel.

   While it's inappropriate to photograph gifts or gift wrapping in small retail shops, you can take pictures of store signs, window displays, colors, shapes, and other intriguing visuals that inspire you to build a thriving business.

21. Market the items in your inventory, like the approved ribbons, paper, or tape that can be purchased as single items.

   As a gift wrapping solution specialist, you create and market a variety of gifts for every occasion.

22. Welcome your website visitors with a beautiful, seasonal wrapped gift featured on your site's home page. Be sure to position the picture so a website visitor sees it immediately when they arrive. This will maintain their attention and encourage them to explore additional pages.

Creating and updating your website is so important to your success that an entire lesson in the online Start Your Own Mobile Gift Wrapping Business course at michellemhensley.com is dedicated to this topic.

23. Connect with your clients each year to gauge their joy factor. You can never take clients for granted. So, staying updated about their preferences is vital to your business.

     You can do this in numerous ways. But speaking with clients face-to-face or by phone is most effective. Text works well today too. Make this about them, not your business. I was speaking with a client while she was placing an order, and she said she was an only child and her father was in hospice. So I spent time encouraging her because I had just lost my mom and have a certification in life and grief coaching. I just took the time to listen and have a good, heartfelt conversation with her. This also gave me an opportunity to send her a little gift to encourage her during this difficult time.

24. Create two- or three-minute videos about your gift wrapping ideas to post on your business's website, YouTube channel, and other social media pages that allow you to upload videos. Adding videos will elevate interest in your offerings, and that will increase followers. It took me a while to start doing this. But finally, at age sixty, I just started and got over my fear of being on video.

     Video ideas include arriving at a trade show to locate products, telling a story from your studio about why you're making a gift basket, and allowing a client to share how your gift wrapping makes the act of gift giving more beautiful and personal.

25. Carry business cards that stand out, and bring small postcards to every networking event you attend. I spend

a lot in this area. We offer high-end and high-quality gift wrapping, so I purchase letterpress business cards.

Not having enough cards on hand is unfortunate when you meet an important person, a potential client, or someone with the ability to order or refer your business. This has happened to me many times, and it is not wise. If I am short on business cards, I give out the postcard with a discount attached to it.

26. Send physical birthday cards to clients. This easy activity enables you to stand out from others who make gifts and opens the door for future business, especially if you decide to grow a corporate gift business with me.

Ask each client for their birth month rather than the actual day, and mail the card at the beginning of the month so the card stays in their sight all month long as a reminder of your thoughtfulness.

I am not a fan of e-cards. They get lost and feel like a last-minute thought. A physical card makes a bigger impact and has a 90 percent open rate.

27. Sponsor local events that allow you to display your business name on banners, chair backs, T-shirts, water bottles, giveaways, and other places that provide exposure and prominence. I did this with a local chamber of commerce. I am not sure if there was a big return on investment, but there can be for sure!

Align yourself with events that are popular, widely publicized, and part of your giving-back mission.

28. Research and find online tools that let you market your business through many social media accounts at once rather than going to each account to post the same information.

This will help you save time and streamline postings. Planoly and Tailwind are two such platforms that let you post marketing messages in one bundle to your Facebook, Twitter, LinkedIn, and Instagram pages.

29. Set a goal each month to submit news about your business to your area's most popular newspaper.

    This strategy can seem outdated, but it's a wise move. Others who wrap gifts may not pursue this free promotional opportunity, which has the potential for print and online distribution.

    You will bring local attention to your gift wrapping, which is a niche, and increase your chance to attract regional, statewide, or countrywide orders.

30. Subscribe to alert systems offered by Google and Yahoo! to receive emailed news updates about what the media prints and designers post worldwide about gift wrapping. It can help you generate new ideas or reach out to someone who is doing something you can support.

    Type "Google Alerts" and "Yahoo Alerts" into any search engine to find each service. Then, set up alerts to receive news every time the phrase "gift wrapping or mobile gift wrapping" (add quotes around the words as shown) appears in online articles.

    These alerts can help you find local designers you don't know and learn how other gift wrap designers and makers market so that you can identify new ways to sell.

31. Look for and send news items of interest to your clients as you search for your own marketing news. This tactic shares news about their profession, industry, or lifestyle.

    It's simple to email links with news clippings or send information by mail. This gesture positions you as a trusted source of valuable data—especially if it is trending and useful for them.

32. Talk to prospective clients (otherwise known as lead nurturing) about your gift wrapping in a way that tells a story about how you made a cool gift wrap or helped make a cool wrap design. This communicates to them the quality of your work.

    The more a story relates to the emotional side of gift giving (sharing joy, happiness, comfort, etc.), the more a potential buyer will be convinced that you are the person who will create a great experience for them too. We created a trendy, beautiful gift wrap for Too Faced Cosmetics that received about a million views on their Instagram account.

33. Create a fifteen- to thirty-second sentence (known as a pitch) to introduce you and your business in a way that makes people want to hear more. This marketing approach is similar to #1 above, but it offers an alternative way of introducing yourself. It also teaches you to know your audience. It's short enough to say in an elevator ride, which is why it is called an "elevator pitch."

    One such pitch might start off with: "I bring owners of multimillion-dollar businesses together to earn more revenue in less time."

    This will need to be cultivated over time, but start creating a story about what led you to start mobile gift wrapping as a business.

    Write down the words that explain how you solve problems through beautiful, trendy gift wrapping and how it sets the recipient apart from all other giving. Practice your introduction again and again so that it's memorable yet natural for you to say. I am big on writing it down and committing it to memory.

34. Choose events wisely when deciding to set up a table or booth to exhibit at businesses and pop-up shops.

Think long and hard as you conduct research to determine if the people who attend each show are interested in having you wrap gifts. One of my gift wrapping coaching clients talked to the owner of her hair salon, which had a little gift shop, about setting up a gift wrapping table. It was a great start for getting her name out there, and she made a little money. Plus, it was her first experience, which was a breakthrough.

35. Listen first and give new connections time to explain what they do before you tell them about your business. Most of all, listen to them. Don't tune out while silently preparing your response. Stephen Covey rightly says, "Seek first to understand, then to be understood."[7]

    Showing genuine interest in another person is the first step to securing a long-term sales relationship.

36. Mail a custom-written letter of reintroduction to clients you have not contacted lately or who have not ordered from you in the past year. Send a brochure, a postcard with a little gift, or lumpy mail. I have an embosser, and I hand-paint my cards. Plus, I add a little gift to the card. Sometimes you are out of sight and out of mind, so this contact is a little reminder to them.

    Connecting with them again through a personalized letter may open the door to new sales from longtime customers who stopped buying for reasons unknown to you.

37. Add a blog to your gift wrapping website. This conversation area is where you share stories about how your gift wrapping brings joy, comfort, happiness, and satisfaction

---

[7] Stephen Covey, *The 7 Habits of Highly Effective People* (New York, NY: Simon and Schuster, 1989).

to clients and recipients. It also encourages feedback from happy clients and potential buyers.

Write your stories (also known as blog posts) in an easy, conversational tone, the same way you'd tell someone the story face to face. People love stories! Look at my website for ideas, below for a list of topics and trends to write about.

Three paragraphs are all you need—the opening, middle, and end. At the end, include a link to the webpage where readers can find the wrapped gift or client work mentioned in the story.

Promote your blog post updates in your newsletter and through social media accounts.

38. Follow your local media, political, and business personalities on Twitter, Facebook, and Instagram. Read what they share, and comment when you see a valid reason to start a discussion, express your viewpoint, or agree with their sentiments.

Such interaction may stand out to the individual and help you make a connection that gets you booked on television or secures a corporate account with a politician or corporate executive.

39. Make connections with local company executives on LinkedIn by asking each person to connect with your profile.

You can do this efficiently through LinkedIn by clicking the Connect button on each person's profile page and sending them a quick note introducing yourself. The Connect button tells the contact nothing about who you are or why you wish to connect, so make sure to write a note stating that you are a local business (location is the common bond) and wish to stay in touch through LinkedIn.

Some people will respond quickly, while others require time due to sporadic viewing of their LinkedIn account. Then, decide how to stay in contact with them through this valuable social media resource.

Bonus

40. Research and refresh your marketing ideas by browsing through consumer and trade magazines from all industries.

    You'll find photographs and articles that provide a wealth of information on how to market your new mobile gift wrapping business in new markets by creating an action plan from the tips found in these publications.

Create Your Own Idea Sheet

Now that you have found marketing options that you're excited to try, write down which ones you'll complete first and those you want to try.

Begin with the relationship with your clients. One client leads to two.

Prior to a market downturn, you want to make sure you continually build on your client base, even if it consists of just one. At the same time, you will want to build your lead list with a lead nurturing program that you set up. Every other part of your business can be fragile, but this is your main important goal. Once you have a client, nurture that person or company. Communicate, love, care for, recognize, and create things for them. Find creative ways to communicate.

Because your list is important, regardless of whether they are leads or clients, you need to keep track of them.

When I started Nifty, I used a good, old-fashioned paper notebook and pen! I did not understand the importance of keeping a great record of both until a few years later. This helped me learn to keep track and write, so it worked for a short while. However, I am here to help you not make the mistakes I did.

Lead and lead nurturing means looking for people who are like your avatar or ICA (ideal client avatar). These are people you feel would be a good fit for a client. A client is someone who has purchased from you. You need to separate these and understand both.

When you get a card or contact information or when someone purchases from you, keep track of this. Collect information on them so you have natural conversations and can get to know them over time.

Let's go back to the CRM (customer relationship management tool). You can start with a basic Google Sheet or your QuickBooks accounting software. This helps you keep track of the notes, what industry they are in, how you met them, and any pertinent information that will help you market to them. This list will grow quickly, so keep good records!

Your goal should be to add at least ten people to your list per week. This list will grow as a result of your good work and good name. Your reputation in this space will help you tremendously. Referrals are the best way to grow.

Make sure you Disneyfy your service! That means you go above and beyond to serve your clients from the start of communication until you walk out the door or deliver their beautifully wrapped packages!

I have quarterly giveaways and two monthly emails that go out. Plus, I sent postcards every two months. I maintain all my information in the CRM called Monday. I've tried several CRMs, but this one seems to work best for Nifty. You need to find creative ways to be essential. If a cut needs to be made, you and your business will not be it.

Be consistent in marketing, have a good message, be present when prospecting, and nurture both your clients and your potential clients. Another principle is people forget so don't stop marketing!

You've got this!

Potential Challenges in Mobile Gift Wrapping

For those who are interested in starting a new business, one of the options is running this effective and profitable small business of mobile gift wrapping.

This works well—sometimes better than a traditional brick-and-mortar store—because the start-up costs are way lower and you can set up shop in an extra room, a small space, a garage, or your vehicle.

But sometimes, the challenges of a mobile gift wrapping business can be the mobile part.

Mobile businesses offer the flexibility to reach clients wherever the business owner can find a parking spot. While donut and ice cream trucks have long exemplified this concept, food trucks have gained popularity in recent years.

Beyond food, there's a diverse array of mobile business ideas. Take Nifty, for instance—a nationwide mobile gift wrapping service. Other mobile ventures include selling coffee, secondhand clothing, shoes, flowers, and crafting supplies. I once hired a mobile hair salon to style my mom's hair, and I found it convenient.

Another big challenge is the discipline side of a low-cost mobile business. You might not take it seriously enough and make it more of a hobby than a business. Make sure that you understand in the beginning that you need to discipline yourself to work on your business every single day.

The Benefits of Staying on the Go

There are several benefits of a mobile gift wrapping business:

- **You have lower start-up and overhead costs:** It's not inexpensive to run a business out of a truck or van. However, you have the blessing of not having to pay rent when you are building your business, along with some of the other maintenance expenses.

- **You are not tied to one location or set hours:** This is why I started Nifty—to work when I could and wanted while still homeschooling teens after my husband passed away.

- **You're flexible:** I still have staff working only when there is a project. I have brick-and-mortar workshops and a large storage unit. It helps to not have staff all the time because it keeps your overhead low.

Challenges of a Mobile Business

Of course, even the best mobile business can face challenges. There may be little room for storage in your vehicle. This means you will be refilling your inventory more frequently than you would in a brick-and-mortar shop. However, this helps keep you prudent in managing your inventory.

Managing your inventory usually requires having funds available whenever you need to buy new supplies to keep your business running. I used my garage, then a room, and then a space I leased at a storage facility. Although the rental space added to my overhead costs, it helped me grow. It can be a challenge to find the best locations. I found one near my shop versus my house, but if you're working from home, then one close to your home is ideal.

You may have a few options when it comes to where you can locate your business at any given time—like the mall or your local hair or nail salon. But you can't be in two places at once.

It's always important to understand the kind of clients you want to attract, so go someplace where they can find you. For example, I will be at a resort club for a spring event where the attendees are high-net-worth individuals and families. This is Nifty's avatar, or ideal client, so it is well worth the time to attend.

Being mobile could also mean you use marketing approaches that are different from what traditional businesses use. Mobile shops can use flyers, trendy postcards, and business cards rather than high-cost TV or radio commercials. It gets you out into the community. Plus, you exercise while walking around your neighborhood businesses.

It is important that you have a presence on social media, whether Facebook, Instagram, or even Pinterest, so you can let customers know where you'll be setting up shop. Reels or stories on Instagram are a great way to share your business and tell people where you are. It also helps the business you happen to be at.

Finally, when you operate a mobile business, you need to make sure it's a vehicle that fits your business needs and can also be a reliable form of transportation. Remember that the cost of gas, vehicle registration, and routine maintenance on the vehicle should be part of your budget and overall plan. If you have a car or van that breaks down, it will be difficult to do business until it gets fixed and is back on the road. For your mobile businesses to start finding success, the first challenge is making sure the vehicle you plan to use will fit your needs so you can show up early and not lose clients as a result of not planning well.

What's Unique When Your Business Is Mobile

For any mobile business, there are things to consider that brick-and-mortar storefront owners don't need to think about. For instance, you may need to pay fees or apply for permits to park your vehicle in certain locations, particularly at large public events. You will need to be aware of any local laws regarding mobile businesses. In some cities, there might be limitations on where you can park or operate and how long you can stay in that location. Mobile business insurance is another important consideration. Like most businesses, you should have liability insurance to protect yourself in case a client gets injured while pursuing your business.

Unlike many traditional businesses, a mobile business will also require auto or commercial insurance since it will have a vehicle on the road for business purposes. Some mobile business owners also have contents insurance, which provides coverage in case merchandise is stolen or damaged. Last but not least, any mobile business owner should keep the weather in mind. In some locations, there can be rainstorms, snowstorms, and delays, so you need to plan accordingly.

After all, it's tough to attract people to a mobile business in the rain or snow. However, in Nifty's case, when it rains or snows or there's another inconvenient weather issue, it is a prime way to secure a new client!

However, with a mobile business like Nifty, you can set up shop inside the client's residence or garage. Or you can work in a commercial client's lobby area or a room that is set aside for your mobile gift wrapping. But if you can tolerate the occasional challenging weather day and meet some of the other unique challenges that come with operating a mobile business, running a mobile business can be fun, rewarding, and profitable for an entrepreneur.

Mobile Gift Wrapping for Different Occasions

Cultural differences can be a challenge if you are unfamiliar with what is acceptable, what not to do, and what you should understand. Try to explore gifting for specific occasions and how you can make a significant impact by incorporating cultural and regional elements into mobile gift wrapping designs.

An Indian Hindu couple hired me to do their wedding wraps, which were extravagant. But there are certain ways to wrap unique cultural themes. You can do a search for unique Indian wraps for weddings. I also created a beautiful gift basket for a gentleman in a C-suite position at Disney that incorporated his religion and culture. Always do your research and prepare ahead of time. These are questions your clients will ask. With a Japanese wrap, for example, they fold the paper down in some cases if it is a bereavement gift because that has a specific meaning in their culture. You can offend them if you don't do it correctly.

One of my clients, Republic Music, requested a cake with a printed picture on it and a bottle of wine wrapped beautifully—but they needed it in London! I reached out to a fellow gift wrapper there and had her help me. So, be resourceful when it comes to serving your clients.

If I did not have experience in a certain type of requested wrap, I learned it!

So, concluding there are pros and cons in most businesses. It is best to be prepared, know what those potential issues might be, and understand the unique challenges of a mobile gift wrapping business. But being able to work in an environment where you can avoid paying for a lease, have a flexible schedule, and enjoy unlimited growth potential, makes mobile gift wrapping one of the most profitable businesses!

CONCLUSION

Becoming the Authority in Mobile Gift Wrapping

My reason for starting Nifty to begin with was all about the word *present*, just like a gift. I wanted and needed to be present—present in my grieving, present with my children because there were still two in high school, and present for my grandchildren. Nifty gave me the opportunity to be present during those difficult and launching years. I am assuming there is a drive and reason for you to want to do the same.

You will deserve to grow your business in many different ways if you truly put the practice and suggestions to work. Anyone can build on their skill set or start from the beginning, and I have taught many people how to wrap professionally.

Know that by following this comprehensive guide, you have gained the knowledge, skills, and confidence you need to excel in the art of starting a successful mobile gift wrapping business. Whether you are seeking to impress loved ones or are an entrepreneur looking to establish a successful business, this book serves as the ultimate resource in becoming an authority in mobile gift wrapping.

I have become the number-one mobile gift wrapping business in the US and serve several types of clients and businesses. Our list of clients includes Van Cleef & Arpels, Versace, men who want to impress their wives or significant others, and several other high-level clients, as well as shut-ins across the nation who have arthritis. I have the opportunity to serve all of them.

Now I am an authority as a mobile gift wrapping business coach. I help women (and men) start and grow a successful small business to create extra income. I teach others through my years of experience—both my ups and my downs. I offer several courses and coaching opportunities. One is designed to help widows create a new identity after loss and financial wisdom. Another helps people master the art of becoming a mobile gift wrapping boss. I am currently working on my next course on how to be successful in the luxury gift basket space.

Thank you for taking the time to read my story of how I grew my mobile gift wrapping business to become number one in the nation.

Cheers to you on your journey! Also, don't forget to check out more resources at michellemhensley.com for the full course or a mini course. Also, follow my podcast and others devoted to the challenges and opportunities available through various businesses.

Michelle

Feel free to reach out to me via email at michelle@michellemhensley.com.

Happy wrapping!

$149

One Hour of Consulting
Code: MHHX2024

This offer includes a one hour in-person or online consultation session with Michelle Hensley, founder and CEO of Nifty Package Co or can go towards the online course.

The 1 hour session can cover any additional business or supply-related questions, marketing ideas, work processes, online and offline business applications that may arise after reading the book.

To book, please send an email to michelle@michellemhensley.com
michellemhensley.com

MICHELLEMHENSLEY.COM

FAQS

Q: How much money will this cost?

A: The cost depends on the items you plan to purchase for your business. Some designers buy enough materials to wrap several gifts, and others decide to start with several designs. Knowing how much you want to experiment will guide you. Also, with the Nifty program, you can purchase a mobile gift wrap case full of your first set of gift wrapping supplies so you can put it in your car for your first wrap!

Q: Can I still wrap gifts if I don't have a separate room for designing?

A: Absolutely! A small space in your home that includes a table and an area to organize products and supplies will give you enough room to begin.

Q: I'm not very organized. Is this business still for me?

A: There are many supplies that help you get organized quickly. Look for plastic bins for stocking supplies, drawers for holding ribbon and scissors, and shelves where you can stack gift wrap paper. You'll become familiar with every item's location so that wrapping gifts is a smooth and easy process.

Q: What if I don't like meeting new people? Can I still be successful?

A: An outgoing personality is an asset in promoting your business. However, you can explore alternatives to face-to-face promotion, such as Internet marketing and print advertising. We talk more about marketing your business in Chapter 6 and truly you can get used to meeting new people so you can grow!

ACKNOWLEDGMENTS

I want to thank my family for putting up with the messy house at times, along with my challenges, tears, worries, and blessings, as they patiently listened to Taylor, Skylar, and Cody. My daughters-in-love, Danielle (Cody) and Halannah (Taylor), supported me in so many ways. Danielle helped me start and launch, offering advice, wisdom, and encouragement. And Halannah was a gift wrapping boss! My grandchildren worked alongside me, playing "Nifty" as they learned to wrap and box, even becoming part of the Nifty team.

A big thank-you to my team, the Nifty Team! They have walked through the ups and downs of exciting and difficult jobs, including the support, fun, tears, and hard work that go into the life of an entrepreneur. They encourage and support like no other. The team has grown in their skill set and professionalism. I cannot relate to those who struggle with their team. They have learned to pivot and challenge when needed. But overall, they've been a huge blessing.

My longtime friend Linda has been beside me, supporting me in all my struggles in life from the nonprofit and so many things in regard to Nifty. There are no words.

My friends and support Dave and Eydie MacInnis. When I was ready to throw in the towel, their practical help, words of wisdom, and listening ear were a godsend!

Lastly and most important for me, I have deep gratitude for my faith in the Lord Jesus Christ. I wanted to give up many times. I was tired and weary. But every single morning for the past twenty-eight years, He changed me, grew me, challenged me, and was silent when I needed help. But He always was there through loss, through joy, through the struggle. My faith is my Rock, my Shelter, and my Strong Tower. I would be nothing without Christ.

Mathew 5:16: "I will let my light shine before men so that they may see your good works and glorify my Father in heaven."

Jeremiah 49:11: "Let the widows trust in me."

Proverbs 14:1: "The wise woman builds."

Made in the USA
Columbia, SC
10 October 2024

43430936R00076